Registration Document 2010-11
Air France-KLM

This Registration Document includes the annual financial report

AUTORITÉ
DES MARCHÉS FINANCIERS
AMF

5.5 Consolidated financial statements

5.5.1 Consolidated income statement

Period from April 1 to March 31, *(In € millions)*	Notes	2011	2010
Sales	5	*23,615*	*20,994*
Other revenues		7	5
Revenues		*23,622*	*20,999*
External expenses	6	(14,555)	(13,197)
Salaries and related costs	7	(7,333)	(7,434)
Taxes other than income taxes		(179)	(216)
Amortization and depreciation	8	(1,624)	(1,640)
Provisions	8	(52)	(35)
Other income and expenses	9	243	238
Income from current operations		*122*	*(1,285)*
Sales of aircraft equipment	10	8	(21)
Other non-current income and expenses	10	756	(326)
Income from operating activities		*886*	*(1,632)*
Cost of financial debt		(455)	(410)
Income from cash and cash equivalents		84	106
Net cost of financial debt	11	*(371)*	*(304)*
Other financial income and expenses	11	(78)	(193)
Income before tax		*437*	*(2,129)*
Income taxes	12	196	586
Net income of consolidated companies		*633*	*(1,543)*
Share of profits (losses) of associates	20	(21)	(17)
Net income from continuing operations		*612*	*(1,560)*
Net income for the period		*612*	*(1,560)*
♦ *Equity holders of Air France-KLM*		*613*	*(1,559)*
♦ Non controlling interests		(1)	(1)
Earnings per share – Equity holders of Air France-KLM (in euros)	14.1		
♦ basic		2.08	(5.30)
♦ diluted		1.76	(5.30)

The accompanying notes are an integral part of these consolidated financial statements.

5.5.2 Consolidated statement of recognized income and expenses

(In € millions)	March 31, 2011	March 31, 2010
Net income for the period	**612**	**(1,560)**
Fair value adjustment on available-for-sale securities		
Change in fair value recognized directly in equity	165	6
Change in fair value transferred to profit or loss	4	-
Cash flow hedges		
Effective portion of changes in fair value hedge recognized directly in equity	952	1,159
Change in fair value transferred to profit or loss	68	532
Items of the recognized income and expenses of equity shares	**(7)**	**10**
Currency translation adjustment	**(25)**	**4**
Tax on items taken directly to or transferred from equity		
Income/(expense) recognized directly in equity	(316)	(518)
Total of other comprehensive income included in the recognized income and expenses	**841**	**1,193**
Recognized income and expenses	**1,453**	**(367)**
♦ **Equity holders of Air France-KLM**	**1,452**	**(370)**
♦ Non-controlling interests	1	3

The accompanying notes are an integral part of these interim condensed consolidated financial statements.

5.5.3 Consolidated balance sheet

Assets (In € millions)	Notes	March 31, 2011	March 31, 2010
Goodwill	15	422	401
Intangible assets	16	695	612
Flight equipment	18	11,040	11,349
Other property, plant and equipment	18	2,111	2,252
Investments in equity associates	20	422	446
Pension assets	21	2,995	2,733
Other financial assets (including €503 million of deposits related to financial leases as of March 31, 2011 and €630 million as of March 31, 2010)	22	1,654	840
Deferred tax assets	12.5	933	942
Other non-current assets	25	156	180
Total non-current assets		**20,428**	**19,755**
Assets held for sale	13	21	93
Other short-term financial assets (including €149 million of deposits related to financial leases and 574 million of investments between 3 months and 1 year as of March 31, 2011 compared respectively to €139 million and €343 million as of March 31, 2010)	22	751	517
Inventories	23	558	537
Trade accounts receivable	24	1,938	2,142
Income tax receivables		6	1
Other current assets	25	1,550	979
Cash and cash equivalents	26	3,717	3,751
Total current assets		**8,541**	**8,020**
Total assets		**28,969**	**27,775**

The accompanying notes are an integral part of these consolidated financial statements.

Liabilities and equity (In € millions)	Notes	March 31, 2011	March 31, 2010
Issued capital	27.1	300	2,552
Additional paid-in capital	27.2	2,971	719
Treasury shares	27.3	(94)	(106)
Reserves and retained earnings	27.4	3,675	2,198
Equity attributable to equity holders of Air France-KLM		*6,852*	*5,363*
Non-controlling interests		54	55
Total Equity		*6,906*	*5,418*
Provisions and retirement benefits	29	1,930	1,432
Long-term debt	30	8,980	9,222
Deferred tax	12.5	511	418
Other non-current liabilities	31	272	818
Total non-current liabilities		*11,693*	*11,890*
Liability related to assets held for sale	13	-	10
Provisions	29	287	696
Current portion of long-term debt	30	1,808	1,825
Trade accounts payable		2,211	2,032
Deferred revenue on ticket sales		2,440	2,340
Frequent flyer programs		806	840
Current tax liabilities		3	11
Other current liabilities	31	2,686	2,597
Bank overdrafts	26	129	116
Total current liabilities		*10,370*	*10,467*
Total liabilities		**22,063**	**22,357**
Total liabilities and equity		**28,969**	**27,775**

The accompanying notes are an integral part of these consolidated financial statements.

5.5.4 Consolidated statement of changes in stockholders' equity

(In € millions)	Number of shares	Issued capital	Additional paid-in capital	Treasury shares	Reserves and retained earnings	Equity attributable to holders of Air France-KLM	Non controlling interests	Total equity
March 31, 2009	**300,219,278**	**2,552**	**765**	**(124)**	**2,429**	**5,622**	**54**	**5,676**
Fair value adjustment on available for sale securities	-	-	-	-	6	6	-	6
Gain/(loss) on cash flow hedges	-	-	-	-	1,179	1,179	4	1,183
Currency translation adjustment	-	-	-	-	4	4	-	4
Net income for the year	-	-	-	-	(1,559)	(1,559)	(1)	(1,560)
Total of income and expenses recognized	**-**	**-**	**-**	**-**	**(370)**	**(370)**	**3**	**(367)**
Stock based compensation (ESA) and stock option	-	-	-	-	24	24	-	24
Dividends paid	-	-	-	-	-	-	(1)	(1)
OCEANE	-	-	-	-	69	69	-	69
Treasury shares (Note 27.3)	-	-	-	18	-	18	-	18
Change in consolidation scope	-	-	-	-	-	-	(1)	(1)
Other	-	-	(46)	-	46	-	-	-
March 31, 2010	**300,219,278**	**2,552**	**719**	**(106)**	**2,198**	**5,363**	**55**	**5,418**
Fair value adjustment on available for sale securities	-	-	-	-	166	166	-	166
Gain/(loss) on cash flow hedges	-	-	-	-	697	697	3	700
Currency translation adjustment	-	-	-	-	(24)	(24)	(1)	(25)
Net income for the year	-	-	-	-	613	613	(1)	612
Total of income and expenses recognized	**-**	**-**	**-**	**-**	**1,452**	**1,452**	**1**	**1,453**
Stock based compensation (ESA) and stock option	-	-	-	-	25	25	-	25
Dividends paid	-	-	-	-	-	-	(3)	(3)
Capital decrease	-	(2,252)	2,252	-	-	-	-	-
Treasury shares (Note 27.3)	-	-	-	12	-	12	-	12
Change in consolidation scope	-	-	-	-	-	-	1	1
March 31, 2011	**300,219,278**	**300**	**2,971**	**(94)**	**3,675**	**6,852**	**54**	**6,906**

The accompanying notes are an integral part of these consolidated financial statements.

5.5.5 Consolidated statements of cash flows

Period from April 1 to March 31, (In € millions)	Notes	2011	2010
Net income for the period – Equity holders for Air France-KLM		613	(1,559)
Non-controlling interests		(1)	(1)
Amortization, depreciation and operating provisions	8	1,676	1,675
Financial provisions	11	(3)	7
Gain on disposals of tangible and intangible assets		(11)	61
Loss/(gain) on disposals of subsidiaries and associates		(13)	-
Gain on WAM (ex Amadeus) operation	10	(1,030)	-
Derivatives – non monetary result	11	(25)	(8)
Unrealized foreign exchange gains and losses, net		33	13
Share of (profits) losses of associates	20	21	17
Deferred taxes	12	(215)	(591)
Other non-monetary items		(209)	143
Subtotal		**836**	**(243)**
(Increase)/decrease in inventories		(10)	(28)
(Increase)/decrease in trade receivables		171	(89)
Increase/(decrease) in trade payables		245	126
Change in other receivables and payables		108	(564)
Net cash flow from operating activities		*1,350*	*(798)*
Acquisitions of subsidiaries and investments in associates, net of cash acquired	37	(33)	(2)
Purchase of property, plant and equipment and intangible assets	19	(2,122)	(2,097)
Proceeds on WAM (ex Amadeus) transaction	10	193	-
Proceeds on disposal of subsidiaries and investments in associates	37	-	-
Proceeds on disposal of property, plant and equipment and intangible assets		977	1,053
Dividends received		8	5
Decrease (increase) in investments, net between 3 months and 1 year		(229)	87
Net cash used in investing activities		*(1,206)*	*(954)*

Consolidated statements of cash flows (cont.)

Period from April 1 to March 31, *(In € millions)*	Notes	2011	2010
Increase in capital		6	-
Purchase of non-controlling interests, of shares in non-controlled entities	37	(13)	(16)
Disposal of subsidiaries without control loss, of shares in non-controlled entities	37	14	3
Issuance of long-term debt		900	2,704
Repayments on long-term debt		(646)	(326)
Payment of debt resulting from finance lease liabilities		(550)	(522)
New loans		(110)	(73)
Repayments on loans		231	151
Dividends paid		(3)	(3)
Net cash flow from financing activities		*(171)*	*1,918*
Effect of exchange rate on cash and cash equivalents and bank overdrafts		*(20)*	*3*
Change in cash and cash equivalents and bank overdrafts		*(47)*	*169*
Cash and cash equivalents and bank overdrafts at beginning of period	26	3,635	3,466
Cash and cash equivalents and bank overdrafts at end of period	26	3,588	3,635
Income tax (paid)/reimbursed (flow included in operating activities)		(32)	(3)
Interest paid (flow included in operating activities)		(435)	(357)
Interest received (flow included in operating activities)		49	79

The accompanying notes are an integral part of these consolidated financial statements.

5.6 Notes to the consolidated financial statements

Note 1 Business description

As used herein, the term "Air France-KLM" refers to Air France-KLM S.A., a limited liability company organized under French law excluding its consolidated subsidiaries.

The Group is headquartered in France and is one of the largest airlines in the world. The Group's core business is passenger transportation. The Group's activities also include cargo, aeronautics maintenance and other air-transport related activities including, principally, catering and charter services.

The limited company Air France-KLM SA, domiciled at 2 rue Robert Esnault-Pelterie 75007 Paris, France, is the parent company of the Air France-KLM group. Air France-KLM is listed for trading in Paris (Euronext) and Amsterdam (Euronext).

The presentation currency used in these financial statements is the euro, which is also the Group's functional currency.

Note 2 Significant events

2.1 Arising during the account period

On April 29, 2010, the company WAM was the subject of an Initial Public Offering (IPO) on the Madrid stock exchange. This operation was executed in two stages:

1. a capital increase reserved to the market, to which the Group did not subscribe;
2. the concomitant sale of a portion of the shares held by the Group.

After the operation, the Group's holding decreased from 22% to 15%. At the same time, the governance of WAM was changed. These two items involved the loss of significant influence for the Group as well

as a change in the valuation method of the remaining shareholding. The impact of this transaction on the Group's financial statements is described in Note 10.

In April 2010, the European air space was closed or significantly disrupted due to a volcanic eruption in Iceland.

2.2 Subsequent events

There has been no significant event since the close of the financial year.

Note 3 Accounting policies

3.1 Accounting principles

3.1.1 *Accounting principles used for consolidated financial statements*

Pursuant to the European Regulation 1606/2002, July 19, 2002, the consolidated financial statements as of March 31, 2011 are prepared in accordance with International Financial Reporting Standards ("IFRS") as adopted by the European Commission ("EU") and applicable on the date these consolidated financial statements were established.

IFRS as adopted by the EU differ in certain respects from IFRS as published by the International Accounting Standards Board ("IASB"). The Group has, however, determined that the financial information for

the periods presented would not differ substantially had the Group applied IFRS as published by the IASB.

The consolidated financial statements were approved by the Board of Directors on May 18, 2011.

3.1.2 *Change in accounting principles*

IFRS standards, Amendments and IFRIC's interpretations applicable effective April 1, 2010

The revised standards IFRS 3 "Business Combinations" and IAS 27 "Individual and Consolidated Financial Statements" have been applied since April 1, 2010.

It has conducted to change the accounting rule concerning the loss of significant influence. Note 10 describes the application of this new accounting rule concerning companies in which the Group has ceased to exercise a significant influence during the financial year together with the associated impact.

The other texts with application effective April 1, 2010 have no impact on the Group consolidated financial statements.

IFRS Standards, amendments and IFRIC's interpretations which came into force for financial statement for accounting periods starting April 1, 2011 and not early applied by the Group

The texts adopted by the European Union as of March 31, 2011 described below, and which came into force for accounting periods starting April 1, 2011, have not been applied early by the Group for the establishment of the consolidated financial statements when this arrangement was possible:

✦ the revised standard IAS 24 "Related party disclosures", applicable for annual periods beginning on or after January 1, 2011;
✦ IFRIC 19 "Financial debts paid by equity instruments", applicable for annual periods beginning on or after July 1, 2010;
✦ the revised interpretation IFRIC 14 "Limit on Defined Benefit Asset Minimum Funding Requirements and their Interaction", applicable for annual periods beginning on or after January 1, 2011.

The Group does not expect any significant impact from the application of these new standards, amendments and interpretations.

Other new standards, interpretations and amendments to existing standards are not applicable to the Group.

3.2   Use of estimates

The preparation of the consolidated financial statements in conformity with IFRS requires management to make estimates and use assumptions that affect the reported amounts of assets and liabilities and the disclosures of contingent assets and liabilities at the date of the consolidated financial statements and the reported amounts of revenues and expenses. The main estimates are described in the following notes:

✦ Note 3.6 – Revenue recognition related to deferred revenue on ticket sales;
✦ Notes 3.13 and 3.12 – Tangible and intangible assets;
✦ Note 3.10 – Financial assets;
✦ Note 3.21 – Deferred tax assets;
✦ Note 3.7 – Flying Blue frequent flyer program;
✦ Notes 3.17, 3.18 and 3.19 – Provisions.

The Group's management makes these estimates and assessments continuously on the basis of its past experience and various other factors considered to be reasonable.

The future results could differ from these estimates depending on changes in the assumptions used or different conditions.

3.3   Consolidation principles

3.3.1   *Subsidiaries*

Companies over which the Group exercises control are fully consolidated. Control is defined as the power to govern the financial and operating policies of an entity so as to obtain benefits from its activities. The financial statements of subsidiaries are included in the consolidated financial statements from the date that control commences until the date the control ceases.

Non-controlling interests are presented within equity and on the income statement separately from Group stockholders' equity and the Group's net income, under the line "non-controlling interests".

The effects of a buyout of non-controlling interests in a subsidiary already controlled by the Group and divestment of a percentage interest without loss of control are recognized in equity. In a partial disposal resulting in loss of control, the retained equity interest is remeasured at fair value at the date of loss of control. The gain or loss on the disposal will include the effect of this remeasurement and the gain or loss on the sale of the equity interest, including items initially recognized in comprehensive income and reclassified to profit and loss.

3.3.2   *Interest in associates and joint-ventures*

Companies in which the Group has the ability to exercise significant influence on financial and operating policy decisions are accounted for using the equity method; the ability to exercise significant influence is presumed to exist when the Group holds more than 20% of the voting rights.

In addition, companies in which the Group exercises joint control by virtue of a contractual agreement are accounted for using the equity method.

The consolidated financial statements include the Group's share of the total recognized gains and losses of associates and joint-ventures from the date the ability to exercise significant influence commences to the date it ceases, adjusted for any impairment loss. Adjustments to the carrying amount may also be necessary for changes in the investor's proportionate interest in the investee arising from changes in the investee's equity that have not been recognized in the investee's profit or loss. The investor's share of those changes is recognized directly in the Group's equity.

The Group's share of losses of an associate that exceed the value of the Group's interest and net investment (long term receivables) in this entity are not accounted for, unless:

✦ the Group has incurred contractual obligations; or
✦ the Group has made payments on behalf of the associate.

Any surplus of the investment cost over the Group's share in the fair value of the identifiable assets, liabilities and contingent liabilities of the associate company on the date of acquisition is accounted for as goodwill and included in the book value of the investment accounted for using the equity method.

The investments in which the Group has ceased to exercise significant influence or joint control are no longer consolidated and are valued at their fair value on the date of withdrawal from the consolidation scope.

3.3.3 Intra-group operations

All intra-group balances and transactions, including income, expenses and dividends are eliminated in full. Profits and losses resulting from intra-group transactions that are recognized in assets are eliminated in full.

Gains and losses realized on internal sales with associates and jointly-controlled entities are eliminated, to the extent of the Group's interest in the entity, providing there is no impairment.

3.3.4 Closing date

With the exception of a few non-significant subsidiaries and equity affiliates with a December 31 closing date, all Group companies are consolidated based on financial statements for the year ended March 31.

3.4 Translation of foreign companies' financial statements and transactions in foreign currencies

3.4.1 Translation of foreign companies' financial statements

The financial statements of foreign subsidiaries are translated into euros on the following basis:

+ with the exception of the equity for which historical prices are applied, balance sheet items are converted on the basis of the foreign currency rates in effect at the closing date;
+ the income statement and the statement of cash flows are converted on the basis of the average foreign currency exchange rates for the period;
+ the resulting foreign exchange adjustment is recorded in the "Translation adjustments" item included within equity.

Goodwill is expressed in the functional currency of the entity acquired and is converted into euros using the foreign currency rate in effect at the closing date.

3.4.2 Translation of foreign currency transactions

Foreign currency transactions are translated using the exchange rate prevailing on the date of the transaction.

Assets and liabilities denominated in foreign currencies are translated at the rates in effect on the balance sheet date or at the rate of the related hedge for assets resulting from firm commitments documented in fair value hedge relationships.

The corresponding exchange rate differences are recorded in the Group's consolidated income statement. Changes in fair value of the hedging instruments are recorded using the accounting treatment described in Note 3.10. "Financial instruments, valuation of financial assets and liabilities".

3.5 Business combinations

3.5.1 Business combinations completed on or after April 1, 2010

Business combinations completed on or after April 1, 2010 are accounted for using the purchase method in accordance with IFRS 3 revised standard "Business combinations". In accordance with this standard, all assets, liabilities assumed and contingent liabilities are measured at fair value at the acquisition date. The time period for adjustments to goodwill/negative goodwill is limited to 12 months from the date of acquisition, except for non-current assets classified as assets held for sale which are measured at fair value less costs to sell.

Goodwill arising from the difference between the acquisition cost, which includes the potential equity instruments issued by the Group to gain control on the acquired entity and other costs potentially dedicated to the business combination, and the Group's interest in the fair value of the identifiable assets and liabilities acquired is subject to annual impairment tests or more frequently if events or changes in circumstances indicate that goodwill might be impaired.

Costs other than those related to the issuance of debt or equity securities are recognized immediately as an expense when incurred.

For each acquisition, the Group has the option of using the "full" goodwill method, where goodwill is calculated by taking into account the fair value of non-controlling interests at the acquisition date rather than their proportionate interest in the fair value of the assets and liabilities of the acquiree.

Should the fair value of identifiable assets acquired and liabilities assumed exceed the cost of acquisition, the resulting negative goodwill is recognized immediately in the income statement.

Contingent considerations or earn-outs are recorded in equity if contingent payment is settled by delivery of a fixed number of the acquirer's equity instrument. In all other cases, they are recognized in liabilities related to business combinations. Contingent payments or earn-outs are measured at fair value at the acquisition date. This initial measurement is subsequently adjusted through goodwill only when additional information is obtained after the acquisition date about facts and circumstances that exists at that date. Such adjustment is made only during the 12 months measurement period that follows the acquisition date. All other subsequent adjustment which does not meet these criteria is recorded as a receivable or payable through income statement.

In a step acquisition, the previously-held equity interest in the acquiree is remeasured at its acquisition-date fair value. The difference between the fair value and the net book value must be accounted in profit or loss as well as elements previously recognized in other comprehensive income.

3.5.2 *Business combination carried out before April 1, 2010*

Business combinations carried out before April 1, 2010 are accounted for using the purchase method in accordance with IFRS 3 "Business combinations". In accordance with this standard, all assets, liabilities assumed and contingent liabilities are measured at fair value at the acquisition date. The time period for adjustments to goodwill/negative goodwill is limited to 12 months from the date of acquisition.

Assets meeting the criteria of IFRS 5 "Non-current assets held for sale and discontinued operations", as described in Note 3.22, are recorded at the lower of their net book value and their fair value less costs to sell.

Goodwill arising from the difference between the acquisition cost, which includes the potential equity instruments issued by the Group to gain control on the acquired entity and other costs potentially dedicated to the business combination, and the Group's interest in the fair value of the identifiable assets and liabilities acquired is subject to annual impairment tests or more frequently if events or changes in circumstances indicate that goodwill might be impaired.

Should the fair value of identifiable assets acquired and liabilities assumed exceed the cost of acquisition, the resulting negative goodwill is recognized immediately in the income statement.

3.6 Sales

Sales related to air transportation operations are recognized when the transportation service is provided, net of any discounts granted. Transportation service is also the trigger for the recognition of external expenses, such as the commissions paid to agents.

Upon issuance, both passenger and cargo tickets are recorded as "Deferred revenue on ticket sales".

Sales relating to the value of tickets that have been issued, but which will never be used, are recognized as revenues at issuance. The amounts recognized are based on a statistical analysis, which is regularly updated.

Sales on third-party maintenance contracts are recorded based on the stage of completion.

3.7 Loyalty programs

The two sub-groups Air France and KLM have a common frequent flyer program "Flying Blue". This program allows members to acquire "miles" as they fly on Air France, KLM or with other partner companies. These miles entitle members to a variety of benefits such as free flights with the two companies.

In accordance with the IFRIC 13 "Loyalty programmes", these "miles" are considered distinct elements from a sale with multiple elements and one part of the price of the initial sale of the airfare is allocated to these "miles" and deferred until the Groups commitments relating to these "miles" have been met.

The deferred amount due in relation to the acquisition of miles by members is estimated:

+ according to the fair value of the "miles", defined as the amount at which the benefits can be sold separately;
+ after taking into account the redemption rate, corresponding to the probability that the miles will be used by members, using a statistical method.

With regards to the invoicing of other partners in the program, the margins realized on sales of "miles" by the sub-groups Air France and KLM to other partners is recorded immediately in the income statement.

3.8 Distinction between income from current operations and income from operating activities

The Group considers it relevant to the understanding of its financial performance to present on the face of the income statement a subtotal within the income from operating activities. This subtotal, named "Income from current operations", excludes those elements that have little predictive value due to their nature, frequency and/or materiality, as defined in the No. 2009-R.03 recommendation from the National Accounting Council.

Such elements can be divided into three categories:

+ elements that are both very infrequent and significant, such as the recognition in the income statement of negative goodwill;
+ elements that impact the understanding of the Group's financial performance and do not contribute to the establishment of reliable future projections, such as the sales of aircraft equipment and disposals of other assets;
+ elements that are by nature unpredictable and non-recurring, if they are significant such as restructuring costs or gains/(losses) resulting from specific transactions. The Group considers that materiality must be assessed not only by comparing the amount concerned with the income/(loss) from operating activities of the period, but also in terms of changes in the item from one period to the other.

3.9 Earnings per share

Earnings per share are calculated by dividing net income attributable to the equity holders of Air France-KLM by the average number of shares outstanding during the period. The average number of shares outstanding does not include treasury shares.

Diluted earnings per share are calculated by dividing the net income attributable to the equity holders of Air France-KLM adjusted for the effects of dilutive instrument exercise, by the average number of shares outstanding during the period, adjusted for the effect of all potentially-dilutive ordinary shares.

3.10 Financial instruments, valuation of financial assets and liabilities

3.10.1 Valuation of trade receivables and non-current financial assets

Trade receivables, loans and other non-current financial assets are considered to be assets issued by the Group and are recorded at fair value then, subsequently, using the amortized cost method less impairment losses, if any. The purchases and sales of financial assets are accounted for as of the transaction date.

3.10.2 Investments in debt and equity securities

Investments in debt and equity securities qualifying as assets available for sale are stated at fair value in the Group's balance sheet. For publicly-traded securities, the fair value is considered to be the market price. For other securities, if the fair value cannot be reliably estimated, it equals the acquisition cost less impairment, if any.

Potential gains and losses, except for impairment charges, are recorded in a specific component of equity "Derivatives and available for sale securities reserves". If there is an indication of impairment of the financial asset, the amount of the loss is recorded in the income statement for the period.

3.10.3 Derivative financial instruments

The Group uses various derivative financial instruments to hedge its exposure to the risks of exchange rates, changes in interest rates or fuel prices.

Forward currency contracts and options are used to cover exposure to exchange rates. For firm commitments, the unrealized gains and losses on these financial instruments are included in the carrying value of the hedged asset or liability.

The Group also uses rate swaps to manage its exposure to interest rate risk. Most of the swaps traded convert floating-rate debt to fixed-rate debt.

Finally, exposure to the fuel risk is hedged by swaps or options on jet fuel, diesel or Brent.

Most of these derivatives are classified as hedging instruments if the derivative is eligible as a hedging instrument and if the hedging contracts are documented as required by IAS 39 "Financial instruments: recognition and measurement".

These derivative instruments are recorded on the Group's consolidated balance sheet at their fair value. The method of accounting for changes in fair value depends on the classification of the derivative instruments. There are three classifications:

✦ *derivatives classified as fair value hedge*: changes in the derivative fair value are recorded through the income statement and offset within the limit of its effective portion against the changes in the fair value of the underlying item (assets, liability or firm commitment), which are also recognized as earnings;

✦ *derivatives classified as cash flow hedge*: the changes in fair value are recorded in equity for the effective portion and are reclassified as income when the hedged element affects earnings. The ineffective portion is recorded as financial income or financial losses;

✦ *derivatives classified as trading*: changes in the derivative fair value are recorded as financial income or losses.

3.10.4 Convertible bonds

Convertible bonds are financial instruments comprised of two components: a bond component recorded as debt and a stock component recorded in equity. The bond component is equal to the discounted value of all coupons due for the bond at the rate of a simple bond that would have been issued at the same time as the convertible bond. The value of the stock component recorded in the Group's equity is calculated by the difference between such value and the bond's nominal value at issue. The difference between the financial expense recorded and the amounts effectively paid out is added, at each closing, to the amount of the debt component so that, at maturity, the amount to be repaid if there is no conversion equals the redemption price.

3.10.5 Financial assets, cash and cash equivalents

Financial assets at fair value through profit and loss

Financial assets are made up of financial assets at fair value through profit and loss (French mutual funds such as SICAV and FCP, certificates, etc.) that the Group intends to sell in the near term to realize a capital gain, or that are part of a portfolio of identified financial instruments managed collectively and for which there is evidence of a practice of short-term profit taking. They are classified in the balance sheet as current financial assets. Furthermore, the Group opted not to designate any asset at fair value through the income statement.

Cash and cash equivalents

Cash and cash equivalents are short-term, highly liquid investments that are readily convertible to known amounts of cash and which are subject to an insignificant risk of change in value.

3.10.6 *Long-term debt*

Long-term debt is recognized initially at fair value. Subsequent to the initial measurement, long-term debt is recorded at amortized cost calculated using the effective interest rate. Under this principle, any redemption and issue premiums are recorded as debt in the balance sheet and amortized as financial income or expense over the life of the loans.

In addition, long-term debt documented in the context of fair value hedging relationships is revalued at the fair value for the risk hedged, i.e. the risk related to the fluctuation in interest rates. Changes in fair value of the hedged debt are recorded symmetrically in the income statement for the period with the change in fair value of the hedging swaps.

3.10.7 *Fair value hierarchy*

The table presenting a breakdown of financial assets and liabilities categorized by value (See Note 32.4) meets the amended requirements of IFRS 7 "Financial instruments: Disclosures". The fair values are classed using a scale which reflects the nature of the market data used to make the valuations. This scale has three levels of fair value:

+ **level 1:** Fair value calculated from the exchange rate/price quoted on the active market for identical instruments;
+ **level 2:** Fair value calculated from valuation techniques based on observable data such as active prices or similar liabilities or scopes quoted on the active market;
+ **level 3:** Fair value calculated from valuation techniques which rely completely or in part on non-observable data such as prices on an inactive market or the valuation on a multiples basis for non-quoted securities.

3.11 **Goodwill**

Goodwill represents the excess of the cost of a business combination over the acquirer's interest in the fair value of the acquired identifiable assets, liabilities and contingent liabilities.

For acquisitions prior to April 1, 2004, goodwill is included on the basis of its deemed cost, which represents the amount recorded under French GAAP. The classification and accounting treatment of business combinations that occurred prior to April 1, 2004 was not modified at the time international standards were adopted, on April 1, 2004, in accordance with IFRS 1 "First-time adoption of international financial reporting standards".

Goodwill is valued in the functional currency of the entity acquired. It is recorded as an asset in the balance sheet.

It is not amortized and is tested for impairment annually and at any point during the year when an indicator of impairment exists. As discussed in Note 3.14, once recorded the impairment may not subsequently be reversed.

When the acquirer's interest in the net fair value of the identifiable assets, liabilities and contingent liabilities acquired exceeds the acquisition cost, there is negative goodwill which is recognized and immediately reversed in the Group's income statement.

At the time of the sale of a subsidiary, an equity affiliate or a jointly-controlled entity, the amount of the goodwill attributable to the entity sold is included in the calculation of the income from the sale.

3.12 **Intangible assets**

Intangible assets are recorded at initial cost less accumulated amortization and any accumulated impairment losses.

Software development costs are capitalized and amortized over their useful lives. The Group has the necessary tools to enable the tracking by project of all the stages of development, and particularly the internal and external costs directly related to each project during its development phase.

Identifiable intangible assets acquired with a finite useful life are amortized over their useful life from the date they are available for use.

Identifiable intangible assets acquired with an indefinite useful life are not amortized but tested annually for impairment or whenever there is an indication that the intangible asset may be impaired. If necessary, an impairment as described in Note 3.14 is recorded.

Intangible assets with a finite useful life are amortized on a straight line basis over the following periods:

+ software   1 to 5 years;
+ customer relationships   5 to 12 years.

3.13 **Property, plant and equipment**

3.13.1 *Principles applicable*

Property, plant and equipment are recorded at the acquisition or manufacturing cost, less accumulated depreciation and any accumulated impairment losses.

The financial interest attributed to progress payments made on account of aircraft and other significant assets under construction is capitalized and added to the cost of the asset concerned. Insofar as investment installments are not financed by specific loans, the Group uses the average interest rate on the current unallocated loans of the period.

Maintenance costs are recorded as expenses during the period when incurred, with the exception of programs that extend the useful life of the asset or increase its value, which are then capitalized (e.g. maintenance on airframes and engines, excluding parts with limited useful lives).

3.13.2 Flight equipment

The purchase price of aircraft equipment is denominated in foreign currencies. It is translated at the exchange rate at the date of the transaction or, if applicable, at the hedging price assigned to it. Manufacturers' discounts, if any, are deducted from the value of the related asset.

Aircraft are depreciated using the straight-line method over their average estimated useful life of 20 years, assuming no residual value.

During the operating cycle, in developing fleet replacement plans, the Group reviews whether the amortizable base or the useful life should be adjusted and, if necessary, determines whether a residual value should be recognized.

Any major airframes and engines (excluding parts with limited useful lives) are treated as a separate asset component with the cost capitalized and depreciated over the period between the date of acquisition and the next major overhaul.

Aircraft components enable the use of the fleet to be ensured are recorded as fixed assets and are amortized on a straight-line basis over the estimated residual lifetime of the aircraft/engine type on the world market. The useful life is a maximum of 30 years.

3.13.3 Other property, plant and equipment

Other property, plant and equipment are depreciated using the straight line method over their useful life. Such useful lives are as follows:

+ buildings   20 to 50 years;
+ fixtures and fittings   8 to 15 years;
+ flight simulators   10 to 20 years;
+ equipment and tooling   5 to 15 years.

3.13.4 Leases

In accordance with IAS 17 "Leases", leases are classified as finance leases when the lease arrangement transfers substantially all the risks and rewards of ownership to the lessee. All other leases are classified as operating leases.

The assets held under a finance lease are recognized as assets at the lower of the following two values: the present value of the minimum lease payments under the lease arrangement or their fair value determined at inception of the lease. The corresponding obligation to the lessor is accounted for as long-term debt.

These assets are depreciated over the shorter of the useful life of the assets and the lease term when there is no reasonable certainty that the lessee will obtain ownership by the end of the lease term.

In the context of sale and operating leaseback transactions, the related profit or losses are accounted for as follows:

+ they are recognized immediately when it is clear that the transaction has been realized at fair value;
+ if the sale price is below fair value, any profit or loss is recognized immediately except that, if the loss is compensated for by future lease payments at below market price, it is deferred and amortized in proportion to the lease payments over the period for which the asset is expected to be used;
+ if the sale price is above fair value, the excess over fair value is deferred and amortized over the period for which the asset is expected to be used.

In the context of sale and finance leaseback transactions, any gain on the sale is deferred and recognized as financial income over the lease term. No loss is recognized unless the asset is impaired.

3.14 Impairment test

In accordance with the standard IAS 36 "Impairment of Assets", fixed assets, intangible assets and goodwill are tested for depreciation if there is an indication of impairment, and those with an indefinite useful life are tested at least once a year on December 31.

For this test, the Group deems the recoverable value of the asset to be the higher of market value less cost of disposal and its value in use. The latter is determined according to the discounted future cash flow method, estimated based on budgetary assumptions approved by management, using an actuarial rate which corresponds to the weighted average cost of Group capital and a growth rate which reflects the market hypothesis for the appropriate activity.

The depreciation tests are carried out individually for each asset, except for those assets to which it is not possible to attach independent cash flows. In this case, these assets are regrouped within the CGU to which they belong and it is this which is tested. The CGU relates to different activity sectors of the Group: passenger business, cargo, maintenance, leisure and others.

When the recoverable value of an asset or CGU is inferior to its net book value, an impairment is realized. The impairment of a CGU is charged in the first instance to goodwill, the remainder being charged to the other assets which comprise the CGU, prorated to their net book value.

3.15 Inventories

Inventories are measured at the lower of cost and net realizable value.

The cost of inventories comprises all costs of purchase, costs of conversion and other costs incurred in bringing the inventories to their present condition and location. These costs include the direct and indirect production costs incurred under normal operating conditions.

Inventories are valued on a weighted average basis.

The net realizable value of the inventories is the estimated selling price in the ordinary course of business less the estimated costs of completion and selling expenses.

3.16   Treasury shares

Air-France-KLM shares held by the Group are recorded as a deduction from the Group's consolidated equity at the acquisition cost. Subsequent sales are recorded directly in equity. No gains or losses are recognized in the Group's income statement.

3.17   Employee Benefits

The Group's obligations in respect of defined benefit pension plans and termination indemnities are calculated, in accordance with IAS 19 "Employee benefits", using the projected units of credit method, factoring in the specific economic conditions in each country concerned. The commitments are covered either by insurance or pension funds or by provisions recorded on the balance sheet as and when rights are acquired by employees.

Actuarial gains or losses are recognized in the Group's income statement only if the net cumulative unrecognized actuarial gains and losses at the end of the previous reporting period exceed 10% of the greater of the present value of the defined benefit obligation at that date and the fair value of any plan assets at that date. The exceeding amount is then recognized over the expected average remaining working lives of the employees participating in the plan.

Specific information related to the recognition of some pension plan assets
Pension plans in the Netherlands are generally subject to minimum funding requirements ("MFR") that can involve pension surpluses recognition.

These pension surpluses constituted by the KLM sub group are recognized in the balance sheet according to the IFRIC 14 interpretation "IAS 19 – The Limit on a Defined Benefit Asset, Minimum Funding Requirements and their Interaction".

3.18   Provisions for restitution of aircraft under operating leases

For certain operating leases, the Group is contractually committed to restitute aircraft to a defined level of potential.

The Group accrues for restitution costs related to aircraft under operating leases as soon as the asset does not meet the return condition criteria.

When the condition of aircraft exceeds the return condition as set per the lease arrangement, the Group capitalizes the related amount in excess under "Flight equipment". Such amounts are subsequently amortized on a straight-line basis over the period during which the potential exceeds the restitution condition. Any remaining capitalized excess potential upon termination of a lease is reimbursable by the lessor.

3.19   Other provisions

The Group recognizes a provision in the balance sheet when the Group has an existing legal or implicit obligation to a third party as a result of a past event, and it is probable that an outflow of economic benefits will be required to settle the obligation. The amounts recorded as provisions are discounted when the effect of the passage of time is material.

The effect of the time value of money is presented as a component of financial income.

Restructuring provisions are recognized once the Group has established a detailed and formal restructuring plan which has been announced to the parties concerned.

3.20   Equity and debt issuance costs

Debt issuance costs are amortized as financial expenses over the term of the loans using the actuarial method.

The cost of increase in capital is deducted from paid-in capital.

3.21   Deferred taxes

The Group records deferred taxes using the balance sheet liability method, providing for any temporary differences between the carrying amounts of assets and liabilities for financial reporting purposes and the amounts used for taxation purposes, except for exceptions described in IAS 12 "Income taxes".

The tax rates used are those enacted or substantively enacted at the balance sheet date.

Net deferred tax balances are determined on the basis of each entity's tax position.

Deferred tax assets related to temporary differences and carry forwards are recognized only to the extent it is probable that a future taxable profit will be available against which the asset can be utilized at the tax entity level.

Deferred tax corresponding to fiscal losses are recognized as assets given the prospects of recoverability resulting from budgets and medium term plans prepared by the Group. The assumptions used are similar to those used for testing the value of assets (these are described in Note 3.1.4).

A deferred tax liability is also recognized for the undistributed reserves of the equity affiliates.

Taxes payable and/or deferred are recognized in the income statement for the period, unless they are generated by a transaction or event recorded directly as equity. In such a case, they are recorded directly in equity.

3.22 Non-current assets held for sale and discontinued operations

Assets or groups of assets held for sale meet the criteria of such a classification if their carrying amount will be recovered principally through a sale rather than through their continuing use. This condition is considered to be met when the sale is highly probable and the asset (or the group of assets intended for sale) is available for immediate sale in its present condition. Management must be committed to a plan to sell, with the expectation that the sale will be realized within a period of twelve months from the date on which the asset or group of assets was classified as assets held for sale.

The Group determines on each closing date whether any assets or groups of assets meet the above criteria and presents such assets, if any, as "non-current assets held for sale".

Any liabilities related to these assets are also presented on a separate line in liabilities on the balance sheet.

Assets and groups of assets held for sale are valued at the lower of their book value or their fair value minus exit costs. As of the date of such a classification, the asset is no longer depreciated.

The results from discontinued operations are presented separately from the results from continuing operations in the income statement.

3.23 Share-based compensation

Pursuant to the transitional provisions of IFRS 2 "Share-based payment", only the share-based plans awarded after November 7, 2002, for which the rights did not vest by April 1, 2004, were valued and recorded as salaries and related costs. The other plans are not valued and remain unrecognized. For the Group, the latter only affects the shares-for-salary exchange realized in 1998.

Stock subscription or purchase option schemes are valued at the fair value on the date the plans are awarded.

The fair value of the stock option schemes is determined using the Black-Scholes model. This model takes into account the features of the plan (exercise price, exercise period) and the market data at the time they are granted (risk-free interest rate, market value of the share, volatility and expected dividends).

This fair value is the fair value of the services rendered by the employees in consideration for the options received. It is recognized as salary cost with a corresponding increase to equity over the period for which the rights vest. This compensation cost is adjusted, if applicable, to take into account the number of options effectively vested.

Note 4   Changes in the scope of consolidation

4.1 Acquisitions

No significant acquisitions of subsidiaries occurred during the financial years ended March 31, 2011 and 2010.

4.2 Disposals

Year ended March 31, 2011
On April 29, 2010, the company WAM (Amadeus) was the subject of an Initial Public Offering (IPO) on the Madrid stock exchange. This operation is detailed in Note 10.

Year ended March 31, 2010
No significant disposals of subsidiaries occurred during the financial year ended March 31, 2010.

Note 5   Information by activity and geographical area

Business segments

The segment information by activity and geographical area presented below is prepared on the basis of internal management data provided to the Group Executive Committee Officer, who is the Group's chief operating decision maker.

The Group is organized around the following segments:

Passenger: Passenger operating revenues primarily come from passenger transportation services on scheduled flights with the Group's airline code, including flights operated by other airlines under code-sharing agreements. They also include commissions paid by SkyTeam alliance partners, code-sharing revenues, revenues from excess baggage and airport services supplied by the Group to third-party airlines and services linked to IT systems.

Cargo: Cargo operating revenues come from freight transport on flights under the companies' codes, including flights operated by other partner airlines under code-sharing agreements. Other cargo revenues are derived principally from sales of cargo capacity to third parties.

Maintenance: Maintenance operating revenues are generated through maintenance services provided to other airlines and customers globally.

Other: The revenues from this segment come primarily from catering supplied by the Group to third-party airlines and to charter flights operated primarily by Transavia.

The results, assets and liabilities of the business segments are those that are either directly attributable or that can be allocated on a reasonable basis to these business segments. Amounts allocated to business segments mainly correspond

+ as far as the income statement is concerned, to the current operating income;
+ as far as the balance sheet is concerned, to goodwill, intangible assets, flight equipment and other property, plant and equipment, the share in equity affiliates, some account receivables, deferred revenue on ticket sales and a portion of provisions and retirement benefits.

Other elements of the income statement and of the balance sheet are presented in the "non-allocated" column.

Inter-segment transactions are evaluated based on normal market conditions.

Geographical segments

The Group's activities are broken down into six geographical regions:

+ Metropolitan France;
+ Europe except France and North Africa;
+ Caribbean, French Guiana and Indian Ocean;
+ Africa-Middle East;
+ Americas, Polynesia;
+ Asia and New Caledonia.

Only segment revenue is allocated by geographical sales area.

The carrying amount of segment assets by geographical location and the costs incurred to acquire segment assets are not presented, since most of the Group's assets (flight equipment) cannot be allocated to a geographical area.

5.1 Information by business segment

➤ **Year ended March 31, 2011**

(In € millions)	Passenger	Cargo	Maintenance	Other	Non-allocated	Total
Total sales	19,154	3,176	3,083	1,928	-	27,341
Inter-segment sales	(1,051)	(17)	(2,054)	(604)	-	(3,726)
External sales	**18,103**	**3,159**	**1,029**	**1,324**	**-**	**23,615**
Income from current operations	(44)	69	143	(46)	-	122
Income from operating activities	(44)	69	143	(46)	764	886
Share of profits (losses) of associates	-	-	-	-	(21)	(21)
Net cost of financial debt and other financial income and expenses	-	-	-	-	(449)	(449)
Income taxes	-	-	-	-	196	196
Net income from continuing operations	**(44)**	**69**	**143**	**(46)**	**490**	**612**
Depreciation and amortization for the period	(1,057)	(103)	(304)	(160)	-	(1,624)
Other non monetary items	(71)	(4)	7	(64)	273	141
Total assets	**12,888**	**1,386**	**2,577**	**4,831**	**7,287**	**28,969**
Segment liabilities	6,153	239	577	633	3,544	11,146
Financial debt, bank overdraft and equity	-	-	-	-	17,823	17,823
Total liabilities and equity	**6,153**	**239**	**577**	**633**	**21,367**	**28,969**
Purchase of property, plant and equipment and Intangible assets	**1,552**	**139**	**269**	**162**	**-**	**2,122**

The income from operating activities not allocated mainly corresponds to non-current income and expenses detailed in Note 10.

Non-allocated assets amounting to €7.3 billion are mainly financial assets held by the Group. They comprise financial assets for €1.5 billion, marketable securities of €3.3 billion, deferred tax of €0.9 billion, cash of €0.4 billion and derivatives of €0.9 billion.

Non-allocated liabilities amounting to €3.5 billion, mainly comprise a portion of provisions and retirement benefits of €1.1 billion, deferred tax of €0.5 billion and employee-related liabilities of €1.3 billion and derivatives of €0.6 billion.

Financial debts, bank overdrafts and equity are not allocated.

➤ **Year ended March 31, 2010**

(In € millions)	Passenger	Cargo	Maintenance	Other	Non-allocated	Total
Total sales	17,137	2,455	2,947	1,938	-	24,477
Inter-segment sales	(870)	(16)	(1,991)	(606)	-	(3,483)
External sales	**16,267**	**2,439**	**956**	**1,332**	**-**	**20,994**
Income from current operations	(918)	(436)	81	(12)	-	(1,285)
Income from operating activities	(918)	(436)	81	(12)	(347)	(1,632)
Share of profits (losses) of associates	-	-	-	-	(17)	(17)
Net cost of financial debt and other financial income and expenses	-	-	-	-	(497)	(497)
Income taxes	-	-	-	-	586	586
Net income from continuing operations	**(918)**	**(436)**	**81**	**(12)**	**(275)**	**(1,560)**
Depreciation and amortization for the period	(1,066)	(112)	(279)	(183)	-	(1,640)
Other non monetary items	(230)	(2)	(7)	(46)	(669)	(954)
Total assets	**13,426**	**1,380**	**2,543**	**4,719**	**5,707**	**27,775**
Segment liabilities	5,802	219	608	495	4,070	11,194
Financial debt, bank overdraft and equity	-	-	-	-	16,581	16,581
Total liabilities and equity	**5,802**	**219**	**608**	**495**	**20,651**	**27,775**
Purchase of property, plant and equipment and Intangible assets	**1,543**	**147**	**250**	**157**	**-**	**2,097**

The income from operating activities not allocated mainly corresponds to non-current income and expenses detailed in Note 10.

Non-allocated assets amounting to €5.7 billion are mainly financial assets held by the Group, comprising marketable securities of €3.3 billion, deferred tax of €0.9 billion, cash of €0.5 billion and derivatives of €0.5 billion.

Non-allocated liabilities amounting to €4.1 billion, mainly comprise a portion of provisions and retirement benefits of €1.1 billion, tax and employee-related liabilities of €1.2 billion and derivatives of €1.2 billion.

Financial debts, bank overdrafts and equity are not allocated.

5.2 Information by geographical area

Sales by geographical area

➤ Year ended March 31, 2011

(In € millions)	Metropolitan France	Europe except France, North Africa	Caribbean, French Guiana, Indian Ocean	Africa- Middle East	Americas, Polynesia	Asia, New Caledonia	Total
Scheduled passenger	5,492	5,720	337	1,163	2,941	1,637	17,290
Other passenger sales	333	272	10	58	54	86	813
Total passenger	*5,825*	*5,992*	*347*	*1,221*	*2,995*	*1,723*	*18,103*
Scheduled cargo	338	1,048	34	236	516	824	2,996
Other cargo sales	49	27	4	12	38	33	163
Total cargo	*387*	*1,075*	*38*	*248*	*554*	*857*	*3,159*
Maintenance	610	381	-	-	38	-	1,029
Others	374	891	19	40	-	-	1,324
Total	**7,196**	**8,339**	**404**	**1,509**	**3,587**	**2,580**	**23,615**

➤ Year ended March 31, 2010

(In € millions)	Metropolitan France	Europe except France, North Africa	Caribbean, French Guiana, Indian Ocean	Africa- Middle East	Americas, Polynesia	Asia, New Caledonia	Total
Scheduled passenger	5,242	5,241	328	1,046	2,393	1,239	15,489
Other passenger sales	312	270	10	56	53	77	778
Total passenger	*5,554*	*5,511*	*338*	*1,102*	*2,446*	*1,316*	*16,267*
Scheduled cargo	405	661	25	204	390	628	2,313
Other cargo sales	36	18	4	10	31	27	126
Total cargo	*441*	*679*	*29*	*214*	*421*	*655*	*2,439*
Maintenance	553	362	-	-	41	-	956
Others	350	933	24	25	-	-	1,332
Total	**6,898**	**7,485**	**391**	**1,341**	**2,908**	**1,971**	**20,994**

Traffic sales by geographical area of destination

➤ **Year ended March 31, 2011**

(In € millions)	Metropolitan France	Europe except France, North Africa	Caribbean, French Guiana, Indian Ocean	Africa-Middle East	Americas, Polynesia	Asia, New Caledonia	Total
Scheduled passenger	1,885	4,160	1,234	2,541	4,400	3,070	17,290
Scheduled cargo	6	48	158	600	1,133	1,051	2,996
Total	**1,891**	**4,208**	**1,392**	**3,141**	**5,533**	**4,121**	**20,286**

➤ **Year ended March 31, 2010**

(In € millions)	Metropolitan France	Europe except France, North Africa	Caribbean, French Guiana, Indian Ocean	Africa-Middle East	Americas, Polynesia	Asia, New Caledonia	Total
Scheduled passenger	1,985	3,936	1,173	2,372	3,630	2,393	15,489
Scheduled cargo	4	49	154	476	790	840	2,313
Total	**1,989**	**3,985**	**1,327**	**2,848**	**4,420**	**3,233**	**17,802**

Note 6   External expenses

Year ended March 31, *In € millions*	2011	2010
Aircraft fuel	5,720	4,725
Chartering costs	513	487
Aircraft operating lease costs	831	721
Landing fees and en route charges	1,747	1,707
Catering	554	562
Handling charges and other operating costs	1,303	1,281
Aircraft maintenance costs	1,139	1,072
Commercial and distribution costs	896	854
Other external expenses	1,852	1,788
Total	**14,555**	**13,197**
Excluding aircraft fuel	*8,835*	*8,472*

Note 7 Salaries and number of employees

Salaries and related costs

Year ended March 31, *(In € millions)*	2011	2010
Wages and salaries	5,430	5,406
Net periodic pension costs	185	308
Social contributions	1,761	1,768
Expenses related to share-based compensation	26	27
Other expenses	(69)	(75)
Total	**7,333**	**7,434**

The Group pays contributions to a multi-employer plan in France, the CRPN (public pension fund for crew). This multi-employer plan being assimilated with a French State plan, it is accounted for as a defined contribution plan in "social contributions".

The "other expenses" notably comprise the capitalization of salary costs on aircraft and engine overhaul.

Average number of employees

Year ended March 31,	2011	2010
Flight deck crew	8,662	8,855
Cabin crew	22,498	22,593
Ground staff	70,852	73,273
Total	**102,012**	**104,721**

Note 8 Amortization, depreciation and provisions

Year ended March 31, *(In € millions)*	2011	2010
Intangible assets	58	55
Flight equipment	1,281	1,296
Other property, plant and equipment	285	289
Amortization and depreciation	*1,624*	*1,640*
Inventories	14	3
Trade receivables	(2)	9
Risks and contingencies	40	23
Provisions	*52*	*35*
Total	**1,676**	**1,675**

The amortization changes of intangible and tangible assets are presented in Notes 16 and 18.

The changes in inventories and trade receivables impairment are presented in Notes 23, 24 and 25.

The movements in provisions for risks and charges are detailed in Note 29.

Note 9 Other income and expenses

Year ended March 31, *(In € millions)*	2011	2010
Joint operation of routes	15	59
Operations-related currency hedges	175	156
Other	53	23
Total	**243**	**238**

Note 10 Other non-current income and expenses

Year ended March 31, *(In € millions)*	2011	2010
Sales of aircraft equipment	**8**	**(21)**
WAM (Amadeus) operation	1,030	-
Disposals of subsidiaries and affiliates	13	1
Restructuring costs	(18)	(152)
Loss on aircraft held for sale	(6)	(113)
Other	(263)	(62)
Other non-current income and expenses	**756**	**(326)**

WAM (Amadeus) operation

On April 29, 2010, the company WAM (Amadeus) was the subject of an Initial Public Offering (IPO) on the Madrid stock exchange. This operation was executed in two stages:

1. A capital increase reserved to the market, to which the Group did not subscribe;
2. The concomitant sale of a portion of the shares held by the Group.

After the operation, the Group's holding decreased from 22% to 15%. At the same time, the governance of WAM was changed. These two items involved the loss of significant influence for the Group as well as a change in the valuation method of the remaining shareholding.

As a consequence, consistent with IFRS, since the April 29, 2010 IPO, the shares held by the Group have been valued at their market value (market price).

The overall profit recorded in the income statement amounting to €1,030 million breaks down as follows:

+ gain on disposal of shares: €280 million, including €193 million of cash received;
+ valuation at the market price of the remaining shares held by the Group: €750 million.

After this operation, the WAM (Amadeus) shares held by the Group were reclassified as "assets available for sale" (in "other financial assets non current"). The value of the shares is updated at each closing period as a function of the share price. The counterpart of this revaluation is recorded in the other comprehensive income.

Disposals of subsidiaries and affiliates

No other significant disposals of subsidiaries or affiliates occurred during the financial years ended March 31, 2011 and 2010.

Restructuring costs

Year ended March 31, 2011
Following to the extension of the Air France voluntary redundancy plan, an additional provision amounting to €12 million has been recorded in "other non-current income and expenses".

Year ended March 31, 2010
As of March 31, 2010, the Group recorded a €148 million provision to cover a voluntary redundancy plan. This plan concerned 1,700 posts for its subsidiary Air France. The departures mainly took place in 2010.

Loss on aircraft held for sale

Year ended March 31, 2010
As of March 31, 2010, this line included the impact of the fair value adjustments on ten B747s amounting to €(62) million, the fair value adjustments on 15 Fokker 100s amounting to €(15) million and a €35 million provision corresponding to the indemnities due on two cargo aircraft having been withdrawn from operation.

Other

Year ended March 31, 2011

In Europe, the European Commission announced on November 9, 2010 its decision to impose fines on 14 airlines including Air France, KLM and Martinair related to anti-competitive practices – mainly concerning fuel surcharges. The Commission imposed an overall fine of €340 million on the companies of the Air France-KLM group.

This fine is €127 million higher than the provisions already made by the Group in its accounts. Consequently, an additional "non current expense" has been recorded.

A pension plan was closed in the United States. The impact of this closure amounts to €(26) million.

Note 11 Net cost of financial debt and other financial income and expenses

Year ended March 31, (In € millions)	2011	2010
Income from marketable securities	23	21
Other financial income	61	85
Financial income	**84**	**106**
Loan interests	(291)	(271)
Lease interests	(95)	(122)
Capitalized interests	27	35
Other financial expenses	(96)	(52)
Cost of financial debt	**(455)**	**(410)**
Net cost of financial debt	**(371)**	**(304)**
Foreign exchange gains (losses), net	(33)	(26)
Change in fair value of financial assets and liabilities	(48)	(160)
Net (charge) release to provisions	3	(7)
Other financial income and expenses	**(78)**	**(193)**
Total	**(449)**	**(497)**

The interest rate used in the calculation of capitalized interest is 3.75% for the year ended March 31, 2011 and 3.81% for the year ended March 31, 2010.

The financial income mainly comprises interest income and gains on the sale of financial assets at fair value through profit and loss.

In a decision made on January 8, 2010, Venezuela decided to depreciate its currency, the Venezuelan Bolivar. The measure became effective on January 11, 2010. Based on its monetary outstanding in Venezuela, the Group recorded a foreign exchange loss of €17 million as of March 31, 2010.

The change in fair value of financial assets and liabilities recorded as of March 31, 2011 arose mainly from the variation in the ineffective portion of fuel and foreign currency exchange derivatives amounting to €(34) million, together with the change in value of derivative instruments no longer qualified as hedging amounting to €(11) million.

The change in fair value of financial assets and liabilities recorded as of March 31, 2010 arose mainly from the variation in the ineffective portion of fuel and foreign currency exchange derivatives amounting to €(181) million, together with the change in value of derivative instruments no longer qualified as hedging amounting to €23 million.

Note 12 Income taxes

12.1   Income tax charge

Current and deferred income taxes are detailed as follows:

Year ended March 31, *(In € millions)*	2011	2010
Current tax (expense)/income	**(19)**	**(5)**
(Charge)/income for the year	(19)	(5)
Deferred tax income/(expense) from continuing operations	**215**	**591**
Change in temporary differences	(176)	(202)
Change in tax rates	8	-
CAVE impact	4	(31)
(Use)/recognition of tax loss carryforwards	379	824
Income tax (expense)/income from continuing operations	**196**	**586**

The current tax charge relates to the amounts paid or payable in the short term to the tax authorities in respect of the financial year, in accordance with the regulations prevailing in various countries and any applicable treaties.

During the years ended March 31, 2011 and 2010, the Group recognized a deferred tax asset amounting to €379 million and €824 million respectively, given the gains previously realized and the prospects of recoverability.

Impact of the business tax reform

The 2010 Finance Law voted on December 30, 2009, removed the business tax liability for French fiscal entities from January 1, 2010 and replaced it with the new TEC (Territorial Economic Contribution/*Contribution Économique Territoriale* – CET) comprising two contributions: the LDE (land tax of enterprises/*Cotisation Foncière des Entreprises* – CFE) and the CAVE (Contribution on Added Value of Enterprises/*Cotisation sur la Valeur Ajoutée des Entreprises* – CVAE). The latter is calculated by the application of a rate to the added value generated by the company during the year. As the added value is a net amount of income and expenses, the CAVE meets the definition of a tax on profits as set out in IAS 12.2. Consequently, the expense relating to the CAVE will be presented under the line "tax".

For the financial year ending March 31, 2010 and consistent with the measures set out in IAS 12 "Income taxes", the qualification of the CAVE as a tax on profits led the Group to account for a CAVE expense of €37 million, which corresponds to:

+ a CAVE deferred charge relating to the temporary differences in existence at December 31, 2009. This deferred tax liability will be recovered as the temporary differences are reduced;
+ a CAVE current charge which will be paid in 2010 based on the added value generated during the period ended March 31, 2010.

12.2   Deferred tax recorded directly in equity

Year ended March 31, *(In € millions),*	2011	2010
Cash flow hedge	(316)	(518)
OCEANE	-	(36)
Total	**(316)**	**(554)**

12.3 Effective tax rate

The difference between the standard tax rate in France and the effective tax rate is detailed as follows:

Year ended March 31, *(In € millions)*	2011		2010	
Income before tax		*437*		*(2,129)*
Theoretical tax calculated with the standard tax rate in France	34.43%	(151)	34.43%	(733)
Differences in French/foreign tax rates		(5)		86
Non deductible expenses		316		11
Non-taxable income		-		-
Impact of tax loss carryforwards		27		19
CAVE impact		(15)		37
Other		24		(6)
Income tax expenses	**(44.77)%**	**196**	**27.54%**	**(586)**

The tax rates applicable in France and in the Netherlands were set at respectively 34.43% and 25%. The Dutch tax rate has decreased by 0.5 percentage point starting January 1, 2011.

12.4 Unrecognized deferred tax assets (basis)

Year ended March 31, *(In € millions)*	2011	2010
Temporary differences	31	95
Tax losses	196	401
Total	**227**	**496**

As of March 31, 2011, unrecognized deferred tax assets mainly correspond to a portion of the tax loss carry forwards of Air France group subsidiaries, as well as tax loss carry forwards in certain subsidiaries in the United Kingdom.

In France, tax losses can be carried forward for an unlimited period. In the Netherlands, tax losses can be carried forward until their ninth birthday.

12.5 Deferred tax recorded on the balance sheet

(In € millions))	April 1, 2010	Amounts recorded in income	Amounts recorded in equity	Currency translation adjustment	Reclassifica-tion	March 31, 2011
Flight equipment	(1,039)	(78)	-	-	26	(1,091)
Pension assets	(683)	(50)	-	-	1	(732)
Financial debt	453	36	(236)	-	(3)	486
Other liabilities	387	(31)	-	-	(109)	11
Deferred revenue on ticket sales	206	-	(80)	-	(1)	205
Others	(252)	(41)	-		90	(283)
Deferred tax corresponding to fiscal losses	1,452	379	-	-	(5)	1,826
Deferred tax asset/(liability)	**524**	**215**	**(316)**	**-**	**(1)**	**422**

(In € millions)	April 1, 2009	Amounts recorded in income	Amounts recorded in equity	Currency translation adjustment	Reclassifica-tion	March 31, 2010
Flight equipment	(812)	(174)	(1)	1	(53)	(1,039)
Pension assets	(623)	(59)	-	(1)	-	(683)
Financial debt	442	47	(36)	-	-	453
Other liabilities	911	24	(579)	(2)	33	387
Deferred revenue on ticket sales	209	(3)	-	-	-	206
Others	(254)	(70)	62	-	10	(252)
Deferred tax corresponding to fiscal losses	599	826	-	1	26	1,452
Deferred tax asset/(liability)	**472**	**591**	**(554)**	**(1)**	**16**	**524**

Note 13 Assets held for sale and liabilities related to assets held for sale

Year ended March 31, 2011

As of March 31, 2011, the line "assets held for sale" includes the fair value of 5 aircraft held for sale for an amount of €21 million.

Year ended March 31, 2010

As of March 31, 2010, the line "assets held for sale" included the fair value of 8 aircraft held for sale for an amount of €93 million.

The line "liabilities related to assets held for sale" included pre-payment received for the sale of 4 aircraft classified as "assets held for sale".

Note 14 Earnings per share

14.1 Income for the period – Group share per share

Reconciliation of income used to calculate earnings per share

Year ended March 31, *(In € millions)*	2011	2010
Income for the period – Group share	613	(1,559)
Dividends to be paid to priority shares	-	-
Income for the period – Group share (used to calculate basic earnings per share)	613	(1,559)
Impact of potential ordinary shares:		
♦ interest paid on convertible bonds (net of tax)	44	-
Income for the period – Group share (used to calculate diluted earnings per share)	**657**	**(1,559)**

Reconciliation of the number of shares used to calculate earnings per share

Year ended March 31,	2011	2010
Weighted average number of:		
♦ Ordinary shares issued	300,219,278	300,219,278
♦ Treasury stock held regarding stock option plan	(1,334,312)	(1,679,287)
♦ Treasury stock held in stock buyback plan	(661,716)	(1,199,292)
♦ Other treasury stock	(2,961,300)	(2,965,348)
Number of shares used to calculate basic earnings per share	**295,261,850**	**294,375,351**
OCEANE conversion	78,617,611	-
Number of ordinary and potential ordinary shares used to calculate diluted earnings per share	**373,879,561**	**294,375,351**

14.2 Non dilutive instruments

As of March 31, 2011
Given the trend in the average Air France-KLM stock price during the 2010-11 financial year, non-dilutive instruments related to all the stock option plans described in Note 28.

As of March 31, 2010
Given the trend in the average Air France-KLM stock price during the 2009-10 financial year, non-dilutive instruments related to all the stock option plans described in Note 28 and also to the two OCEANEs described in Note 30.

14.3 Instruments issued after the closing date

No instruments were issued after the closing date.

Note 15 Goodwill

Detail of consolidated goodwill

Year ended March 31, (In € millions)	2011			2010		
	Gross value	Impairment	Net value	Gross value	Impairment	Net value
VLM	168	-	168	168	-	168
UTA	112	-	112	112	-	112
Régional	60	-	60	60	-	60
Aeromaintenance Group	20	-	20	21	-	21
Brit Air	18	-	18	18	-	18
CityJet	11	-	11	11	-	11
SIA Kenya	22	-	22	-	-	-
Others	11	-	11	11	-	11
Total	**422**	**-**	**422**	**401**	**-**	**401**

The goodwill concerns mainly the "Passenger" business.

Movement in net book value of goodwill

Year ended March 31, (In € millions)	2011	2010
Opening balance	**401**	**400**
Acquisitions	22	1
Currency translation adjustment	(1)	-
Closing balance	**422**	**401**

A goodwill was recorded on the acquisition of 60% of SIA Kenya, a subsidiary of Servair group.

Note 16 Intangible assets

(In € millions)	Trademarks and slots	Customer relationships	Other intangible assets	Total
Gross value				
Amount as of March 31, 2009	*316*	*107*	*470*	*893*
Additions	-	-	113	*113*
Change in scope	-	-	-	*-*
Disposals	(1)	-	(10)	*(11)*
Transfer	-	-	1	*1*
Amount as of March 31, 2010	*315*	*107*	*574*	*996*
Additions	-	-	153	*153*
Change in scope	-	-	-	*-*
Disposals	-	-	(20)	*(20)*
Transfer	-	-	(6)	*(6)*
Amount as of March 31, 2011	*315*	*107*	*701*	*1,123*
Depreciation				
Amount as of March 31, 2009	-	*(81)*	*(253)*	*(334)*
Charge to depreciation	-	(12)	(43)	*(55)*
Releases on disposal	-	-	7	*7*
Transfer	-	-	(2)	*(2)*
Amount as of March 31, 2010	-	*(93)*	*(291)*	*(384)*
Charge to depreciation	-	(7)	(53)	*(60)*
Releases on disposal	-	-	13	*13*
Transfer	-	-	3	*3*
Amount as of March 31, 2011	-	*(100)*	*(328)*	*(428)*
Net value				
As of March 31, 2010	315	14	283	*612*
As of March 31, 2011	315	7	373	*695*

Intangible assets mainly comprise:

+ the KLM and Transavia brands and slots (takeoff and landing) acquired by the Group as part of the acquisition of KLM. The intangible assets have an indefinite useful life as the nature of the assets means they have no time limit;

+ software and capitalized IT costs.

Note 17 Impairment

With regards to the methodology followed to test impairment, the Group has allocated each goodwill and intangible fixed asset with an indefinite useful life to Cash Generating Units (CGU), which correspond to their business segments.

As of March 31, 2011, goodwill and intangible fixed assets with an indefinite useful life are attached principally to the "Passenger" CGU for €369 million and €284 million respectively.

The recoverable value of the assets of CGUs has been determined by reference to the value used at December 31, 2010 (no change with regards to December 31, 2009). The tests have been realized for all the CGUs on the basis of a three-year Group plan, approved by the management, and which includes a recovery hypothesis after the slowdown in the economy, allowing the medium-term forecasts made by the Group before the crisis occurred to be achieved.

An annual growth rate of 5% has been applied from the 4th to the 10th year of the test then a rate of 2% has been applied as of the 11th year (rate used to determine the terminal value). These growth rates remain the same as those used for the tests realized at March 31, 2010.

The discount rate of 7% at March 31, 2011 and 2010 corresponds to the Group's weighted average cost of capital.

A discount rate higher than 16% would involve the recognition of an impairment.

Note 18 Tangible assets

(In € millions)	Owned aircraft	Leased aircraft	Assets in progress	Other	Total	Land and buildings	Equipment and machinery	Assets in progress	Other	Total	Total
	Flight equipment					**Other tangible assets**					
Gross value											
Amounts as of March 31, 2009	**10,690**	**4,115**	**1,355**	**1,854**	**18,014**	**2,456**	**1,117**	**237**	**944**	**4,754**	**22,768**
Additions	502	1	1,161	110	1,774	71	62	56	28	217	**1,991**
Disposals	(1,306)	(15)	(116)	(177)	(1,614)	(47)	(35)	(1)	(77)	(160)	**(1,774)**
Changes in consolidation scope	-	-	-	-	-	-	-	-	(4)	(4)	**(4)**
Fair value hedge	-	-	(6)	-	(6)	-	-	1	-	1	**(5)**
Transfer	456	552	(1,481)	149	(324)	96	62	(171)	23	10	**(314)**
Currency translation adjustment	6	-	-	-	6	-	-	-	1	1	**7**
Amounts as of March 31, 2010	**10,348**	**4,653**	**913**	**1,936**	**17,850**	**2,576**	**1,206**	**122**	**915**	**4,819**	**22,669**
Additions	493	7	1,172	142	1,814	34	52	78	34	198	**2,012**
Disposals	(1,127)	(7)	-	(144)	(1,278)	(10)	(47)	-	(66)	(123)	**(1,401)**
Changes in consolidation scope	(2)	-	-	-	(2)	2	5	-	5	12	**10**
Fair value hedge	-	-	59	-	59	-	-	-	-	-	**59**
Transfer	910	135	(1,175)	173	43	40	56	(133)	13	(24)	**19**
Currency translation adjustment	-	-	-	-	-	-	(2)	-	-	(2)	**(2)**
Amounts as of March 31, 2011	**10,622**	**4,788**	**969**	**2,107**	**18,486**	**2,642**	**1,270**	**67**	**901**	**4,880**	**23,366**
Depreciation											
Amounts as of March 31, 2009	**(4,100)**	**(1,022)**	**-**	**(767)**	**(5,889)**	**(1,113)**	**(685)**	**-**	**(643)**	**(2,441)**	**(8,330)**
Charge to depreciation	(855)	(298)	-	(210)	(1,363)	(133)	(88)	-	(68)	(289)	(1,652)
Releases on disposal	293	12	-	196	501	40	32	-	76	148	**649**
Changes in consolidation scope	-	-	-	-	-	-	-	-	3	3	**3**
Transfer	157	132	-	(34)	255	5	11	-	(3)	13	**268**
Currency translation adjustment	(5)	-	-	-	(5)	-	-	-	(1)	(1)	**(6)**

| (In € millions) | Flight equipment | | | | | Other tangible assets | | | | | |
	Owned aircraft	Leased aircraft	Assets in progress	Other	Total	Land and buildings	Equip-ment and machi-nery	Assets in progress	Other	Total	Total
Amounts as of March 31, 2010	*(4,510)*	*(1,176)*	-	*(815)*	*(6,501)*	*(1,201)*	*(730)*	-	*(636)*	*(2,567)*	*(9,068)*
Charge to depreciation	(851)	(299)	-	(142)	(1,292)	(133)	(87)	-	(65)	(285)	*(1,577)*
Releases on disposal	307	7	-	126	440	7	17	-	65	89	**529**
Changes in consolidation scope	-	-	-	-	-	(1)	(4)	-	(4)	(9)	**(9)**
Transfer	(149)	127	-	(71)	(93)	-	-	-	2	2	**(91)**
Currency translation adjustment	-	-	-	-	-	-	1	-	-	1	**1**
Amounts as of March 31, 2011	*(5,203)*	*(1,341)*	-	*(902)*	*(7,446)*	*(1,328)*	*(803)*	-	*(638)*	*(2,769)*	*(10,215)*
Net value											
As of March 31, 2010	5,838	3,477	913	1,121	11,349	1,375	476	122	279	2,252	**13,601**
As of March 31, 2011	5,419	3,447	969	1,205	11,040	1,314	467	67	263	2,111	**13,151**

Aeronautical assets under construction mainly include advance payments and maintenance work in progess concerning engines and modifications of aircraft.

Note 35 details the amount of pledged tangible assets.

Commitments to property purchases are detailed in Notes 34 and 35.

The net book value of tangible assets financed under capital lease amounted to €3,826 million as of March 31, 2011 against €3,820 million as of March 31, 2010.

As of March 31, 2010, the Group recorded an additional write-down amounting to €(67) million in "Other non-current income and expenses" (see Note 10).

Note 19 Capital expenditure

The detail of capital expenditures on tangible and intangible assets presented in the consolidated cash flow statements is as follows:

Year ended March 31, (In € millions)	2011	2010
Acquisition of tangible assets	2,012	1,991
Acquisition of intangible assets	153	113
Accounts payable on acquisitions and capitalized interest	(43)	(7)
Total	**2,122**	**2,097**

Note 20 Equity affiliates

Movements over the period

The table below presents the movement in equity affiliates:

(In € millions)	WAM Acquisition (Amadeus)	Alitalia	Kenya Airways	Other	Total
Value of share in investment as of March 31, 2009	-	330	60	56	446
Share in net income of equity affiliates	-	(13)	(5)	1	(17)
Distributions	-	-	(1)	-	(1)
Change in consolidation scope	-	-	-	4	4
Fair value adjustment	-	21	(10)	-	11
Other variations	-	-	-	-	-
Currency translation adjustment	-	-	3	-	3
Carrying value of share in investment as of March 31, 2010	-	338	47	61	446
Share in net income of equity affiliates	(31)	7	3		(21)
Distributions	-	(1)	(2)		(3)
Change in consolidation scope	-	-	12		12
Fair value adjustment	(9)	3	-		(6)
Other variations	-	-	2		2
Currency translation adjustment	-	(8)	-		(8)
Carrying value of share in investment as of March 31, 2011	298	48	76		422
Market value for listed companies		32			

As of March 31, 2011

KLM holds 26% of the capital of Kenya Airways.

Air France-KLM holds 25% of the capital of Alitalia.

On April 29, 2010, the company WAM (Amadeus) was the subject of an Initial Public Offering (IPO) on the Madrid stock exchange. This operation is detailed in Note 10.

The "share of profits (losses) of associates" includes mainly the share of the loss amounting to €(31) million of Alitalia Group. This corresponds to Alitalia's activity from January 1 to December 31, 2010, its annual closing date being December 31.

As of March 31, 2010

The ownership structure of WAM Acquisition (Amadeus) was as follows: 22.11% Air France, 11.06% Iberia, 11.06% Lufthansa, 50.42% Amadelux Investments and 5.35% management.

KLM holds 26% of the capital of Kenya Airways.

Air France-KLM holds 25% of the capital of Alitalia.

The "share of profits (losses) of associates" for the year ended March 31, 2010 includes mainly the share of Alitalia Group losses amounting to €(13) million. This corresponds to Alitalia's activity from April 1 to December 31, 2009, the company being including in the consolidation scope since March 31, 2009 and its annual closing date being December 31.

Simplified financial statements of the main equity affiliates

The equity affiliates as of March 31, 2011 mainly concern the following companies, in which the Group has a significant influence:

✦ **Kenya Airways**
Kenya Airways is a Kenyan airline based in Nairobi.
✦ **Alitalia**
Alitalia Compagnia Aero Italiana Spa comprises the passenger business of the former Alitalia and the assets acquired with the

acquisition of Air One. This company started trading on January 12, 2009 and serves 79 destinations in Italy and around the world with more than 2,200 flights a week.

The financial information for the principal equity affiliates for the years ended March 31, 2011 and 2010 (excluding consolidation adjustments) is presented below:

(In € millions)	WAM Acquisition (Amadeus GTD)	Alitalia	Kenya Airways
	12/31/2009	12/31/2009	03/31/2009
% holding as of March 31, 2010	22%	25%	26%
Operating revenues	2,461	2,827	657
Operating income	550	(274)	37
Net income/loss	272	(327)	(37)
Stockholders' equity	(278)	723	157
Total assets	**5,562**	**2,980**	**707**
Total liabilities and stockholders' equity	**5,562**	**2,980**	**707**
	-	12/31/2010	03/31/2010
% holding as of March 31, 2011	-	25%	26%
Operating revenues	-	3,225	653
Operating income	-	(107)	17
Net income/loss	-	(168)	19
Stockholders' equity	-	548	192
Total assets	**-**	**2,856**	**706**
Total liabilities and stockholders' equity	**-**	**2,856**	**706**

Other information

The share of WAM Acquisition's income not recorded in the Group's consolidated financial statements amounted to €60 million for the

year ended March 31, 2010. Given the negative net equity after neutralization of the sum reinvested by the Air France-KLM group, its contribution to the consolidated financial statements was nil.

Note 21 Pension assets

Year ended March 31, (In € millions)	2011	2010
Opening balance	**2,733**	**2,499**
Net periodic pension (cost)/income for the period	(71)	(123)
Contributions paid to the funds	331	356
Reclassification	2	1
Currency translation adjustment	-	-
Closing balance	**2,995**	**2,733**

The detail of these pension assets is presented in Note 29.1.

Note 22 Other financial assets

Year ended March 31, (In € millions)	2011		2010	
	Current	Non current	Current	Non current
Financial assets available for sale				
Shares	-	977	-	54
Assets at fair value through profit and loss				
Marketable securities	574	-	343	-
Loans and receivables				
Financial lease deposit (triple A)	103	94	101	197
Financial lease deposit (others)	46	409	38	433
Loans and receivables	15	235	21	212
Miscellaneous financial assets	13	-	14	-
Gross value	**751**	**1,715**	**517**	**896**
Impairment at opening	**-**	**(56)**	**-**	**(55)**
New impairment charge	-	(5)	-	(1)
Use of provision	-	-	-	-
Impairment at closing	**-**	**(61)**	**-**	**(56)**
Total	**751**	**1,654**	**517**	**840**

Financial assets available for sale are as follows:

In € millions	Fair Value	% interest	Stockholder's equity	Net income	Stock price (in €)	Closing date
As of March 31, 2011						
Amadeus*	920	15.23%	767	384	13.50	December 2010
Club Med*	10	2.00%	516	(14)	15.20	October 2010
Voyages Fram	9	8.71%	108	(6)	NA	December 2010
Others	38	-	-	-		
Total	**977**					
As of March 31, 2010						
Club Med*	9	2.00%	492	(53)	13.615	October 2009
Voyages Fram	9	8.71%	131	9	NA	December 2009
Others	36	-	-	-	-	-
Total	**54**					

* Listed company.

Assets at fair value through profit and loss mainly comprise shares in mutual funds that do not meet the "cash equivalents" definition.

Loans and receivables mainly include deposits on flight equipment made within the framework of operating and capital leases.

Note 23 Inventory and work in progress

Year ended March 31, (In € millions)	2011	2010
Aeronautical spare parts	582	556
Other supplies	144	137
Production work in progress	6	7
Gross value	**732**	**700**
Opening valuation allowance	**(163)**	**(166)**
Charge to allowance	(21)	(12)
Use of allowance	7	9
Releases of allowance no longer required	-	-
Reclassification	3	6
Closing valuation allowance	**(174)**	**(163)**
Net value of inventory	**558**	**537**

Note 24 Trade accounts receivable

Year ended March 31, (In € millions)	2011	2010
Airlines	459	489
Other clients:		
♦ Passenger	873	1,004
♦ Cargo	409	324
♦ Maintenance	186	276
♦ Other	94	138
Gross value	**2,021**	**2,231**
Opening valuation allowance	*(89)*	*(86)*
Charge to allowance	(14)	(22)
Use of allowance	15	13
Currency translation adjustment	1	
Reclassification	4	6
Closing valuation allowance	*(83)*	*(89)*
Net value	**1,938**	**2,142**

Note 25 Other assets

Year ended March 31, (In € millions)	2011		2010	
	Current	Non current	Current	Non current
Suppliers with debit balances	119	-	74	-
State receivable	86	-	89	-
Derivative instruments	808	138	339	170
Prepaid expenses	259	18	242	9
Other debtors	280	-	239	1
Gross value	**1,552**	**156**	**983**	**180**
Opening valuation allowance	*(4)*	**-**	*(6)*	**-**
Charge to allowance	-	-	(1)	-
Use of allowance	1	-	1	-
Reclassification	1	-	2	-
Closing valuation allowance	*(2)*	**-**	*(4)*	**-**
Net realizable value of other assets	**1,550**	**156**	**979**	**180**

The derivative instruments did not comprise any currency hedges on financial debt as of March 31, 2011 and 2010.

Note 26 Cash, cash equivalents and bank overdrafts

Year ended March 31, *(In € millions)*	2011	2010
Mutual funds (SICAV) (assets at fair value through profit and loss)	3,219	3,171
Bank deposits (assets at fair value through profit and loss)	124	123
Cash in hand	374	457
Total cash and cash equivalents	***3,717***	***3,751***
Bank overdrafts	(129)	(116)
Cash, cash equivalents and bank overdrafts	***3,588***	***3,635***

Note 27 Equity attributable to equity holders of Air France-KLM SA

27.1 Issued capital

As of March 31, 2011, the issued capital of Air France-KLM comprised 300,219,278 fully paid-up shares. Each share is entitled to one vote.

The change in the number of issued shares is as follows:

On August 5, 2010, a capital reduction operation amounting to €2,252 million took place. Since that date, the nominal value of each share has been €1 compared with €8.50 previously.

As of March 31, *(In number of shares)*	2011	2010
At the beginning of the period	***300,219,278***	***300,219,278***
Issuance of shares for OCEANE conversion	-	-
At the end of the period	***300,219,278***	***300,219,278***
Of which:		
♦ number of shares issued and paid up	300,219,278	300,219,278
♦ number of shares issued and not paid up	-	-

The shares comprising the issued capital of Air France-KLM are subject to no restriction nor priority concerning dividend distribution or reimbursement of the issued capital.

Authorized stock

The Extraordinary Shareholders' Meeting of July 8, 2010, authorized the Board of Directors, for a period of 26 months from the date of the meeting, to issue shares and/or other securities giving immediate or future rights to Air France-KLM capital limited to a total maximum nominal amount of €120 million.

Breakdown of share capital and voting rights

The breakdown of share capital and voting rights is as follows:

	% of capital		% of voting rights	
Year ended March 31,	**2011**	**2010**	**2011**	**2010**
French State	16%	16%	16%	16%
Employees and former employees	10%	12%	10%	12%
Treasury shares	2%	2%	-	-
Other	72%	70%	74%	72%
Total	**100%**	**100%**	**100%**	**100%**

The item "Employees and former employees" includes shares held by employees and former employees identified in funds or by a Sicovam code.

Other securities giving access to common stock
OCEANE
Please refer to Note 30.2.

27.2 Additional paid-in capital

Additional paid-in capital represents the difference between the nominal value of equity securities issued and the value of contributions in cash or in kind received by Air France-KLM.

Year ended March 31, *(In € millions)*	**2011**	**2010**
Other paid-in capital	2,971	719
Total	**2,971**	**719**

27.3 Treasury shares

	Treasury shares	
	Number	**In € millions**
March 31, 2009	**5,889,461**	**(124)**
Change in the period	(158,987)	18
March 31, 2010	**5,730,474**	**(106)**
Change in the period	(1,180,562)	12
March 31, 2011	**4,549,912**	**(94)**

As of March 31, 2011, Air France-KLM held 3,433,492 of its own shares (including 360,000 within the framework of the liquidity agreement), acquired pursuant to the annual authorizations granted by the Shareholders' Meeting. As of March 31, 2011, the Group also held 1,116,420 of its own shares for KLM stock option programs. All these treasury shares are classified as a reduction of equity.

27.4 Reserves and retained earnings

Year ended March 31, *(In € millions)*	2011	2010
Legal reserve	70	70
Distributable reserves	1,032	1,064
Derivatives reserves	363	(325)
Available for sale securities reserves	173	7
Other reserves	1,424	2,941
Net income (loss) – Group share	613	(1,559)
Total	**3,675**	**2,198**

As of March 31, 2011, the legal reserve of €70 million represented 23% of Air France-KLM's issued capital. French company law requires that a limited company (*société anonyme*) allocates 5% of its unconsolidated statutory net income each year to this legal reserve until it reaches 10% of the Group's issued capital. The amount allocated to this legal reserve is deducted from the distributable income for the current year.

The legal reserve of any company subject to this requirement may only be distributed to shareholders upon liquidation of the company.

Note 28 Share-based compensation

28.1 Outstanding share-based compensation plans and other plans as of March 31, 2011

Plans	Grant date	Number of shares granted	Start date for option exercise	Date of expiry	Exercise price *(in €)*	Number of options exercised as of 03/31/2011
Stock-option plans						
KLM	07/26/2005	390,609	07/31/2005	07/16/2010	13.11	3,500
KLM	07/26/2006	411,105	07/31/2006	07/26/2011	17.83	-
KLM	07/27/2007	428,850	07/31/2007	07/25/2012	34.21	-

Other plans

Plans	Grant date	Number of shares granted	Date of expiry	Exercise price *(in €)*	Number of shares exercised as of 03/31/2011
Air France – ESA* 1998 pilots	05/01/1999	15,023,251	05/31/1999	14.00	15,023,251
Air France – KLM – ESA* 2003	02/01/2005	12,612,671	02/21/2005	14.00	12,612,671

* *ESA: shares-for-salary exchange.*

28.2   Changes in options

	Average exercise price (in €)	Number of options
Options outstanding as of March 31, 2009	**20.30**	**1,465,686**
Of which: options exercisable at March 31, 2009	*20.30*	*1,465,686*
Options forfeited during the period	14.25	(322,504)
Options exercised during the period	-	-
Options granted during the period	-	-
Options outstanding as of March 31, 2010	**22.00**	**1,143,182**
Of which: options exercisable at March 31, 2010	*22.00*	*1,143,182*
Options forfeited during the period	13.49	(374,966)
Options exercised during the period	-	-
Options granted during the period	-	-
Options outstanding as of March 31, 2011	**26.16**	**768,216**
Of which: options exercisable at March 31, 2011	*26.16*	*768,216*

28.3   Price range of available options as of March 31, 2011

Range of exercise prices per share	Number of options	Weighted average remaining life (years)	Weighted average exercise price per share (in €)
From 15 to 20 euros per share	377,699	0.32	17.83
From 20 to 35 euros per share	390,517	1.34	34.21
Total	**768,216**	**0.84**	**26.16**

28.4   Description of the plans

KLM stock-option plans

Prior to the combination with Air France, members of the Management Board and the key executives of KLM had been granted KLM stock options. Within the combination agreement between KLM and Air France, stock-options and SAR (Share Appreciation Rights) that were not exercised during the operation were modified on May 4, 2004, so that their holders could purchase Air France-KLM shares and SARs attached to Air France-KLM shares. The shares held by KLM within this plan were converted into Air France-KLM shares and transferred to a foundation whose sole purpose is their retention until the stock options are exercised or forfeited.

The vesting conditions of the options granted by KLM on July 2007, 2006 and 2005 are such that one third of the options vest at grant date with a further one third after one and two years, respectively. Vesting is conditional on KLM achieving predetermined non-market-dependent performance criteria.

Air France 1998 shares-for-salary exchange for pilots

On October 28, 1998, Air France signed an agreement granting Air France shares to pilots in return for a reduction in salary (these shares being granted by the French State, the major shareholder at the time). The offer was launched on May 1, 1999 and closed on May 31, 1999. By the end of the offer, 15,023,251 shares were allocated to pilots. Payment for these shares, priced at €14, was to be made through a reduction in salary spread over (i) a 7-year period for 10,263,001 shares and (ii) the remaining career of the pilots for the remaining 4,760,250 shares.

In accordance with the transitional provisions of IFRS 2 "Share-based payments", only plans granted after November 7, 2002 and not yet vested as of April 1, 2004 have been valued and recorded as salary expense. IFRS 2 is therefore not applicable to this plan.

Air France 2003 shares-for-salary exchange

On February 1, 2005, the Group launched a shares-for-salary exchange scheme, in which all Air France employees residing in France were offered the opportunity to purchase Air France-KLM shares at a price of €14 per share in exchange for wage concessions over a 6-year period. The offer was limited to a maximum of 13,186,853 ordinary shares. At the date the offer was closed, i.e. February 21, 2005, Air France employees had acquired 12,612,671 Air France-KLM shares.

These shares were granted by the French State, the largest Air France-KLM shareholder, subject to a €110 million payment made by the Group in April 2007.

The wage concessions cover the period from May 2005 to May 2011.

In the event an employee leaves the Group prior to the end of the 6-year period, the unvested and irredeemable shares are returned to Air France which, in turn, returns them to the French State. The fair value of the services provided under the shares-for-salary exchange scheme was calculated on the basis of the market price of the Air France-KLM share on the date the offer was closed, namely €14.30 and amounts to €180 million. The corresponding salary expense covers the acquisition period of voting rights from May 2005 to May 2011. Each installment, corresponding to the annual decrease of salary, is treated as a separate award. The Shares-for Salary Exchange 2003 plan share-based payment is therefore recognized on a straight-line basis over the requisite service period for each separately-vested portion.

KLM SARs plan

During the periods ending March 31, 2011, 2010 and 2009, Share Appreciation Rights (SARs) were granted by KLM, corresponding to shares-based plans and paid in cash.

Plans	Grant date	Number of SARs granted	Start date for SARs exercise	Date of expiry	Number of SARs exercised as of 03/31/2011
KLM	07/01/2008	153,080	07/01/2008	07/01/2013	-
KLM	07/01/2009	136,569	07/01/2009	07/01/2014	-
KLM	07/01/2010	145,450	07/01/2010	07/01/2015	-

The changes in SARs were as follows:

	Number of SARs
SARs outstanding as of March 31, 2009	**151,880**
Of which: SARs exercisable at March 31, 2009	*49,826*
SARs forfeited during the period	(45,389)
SARs exercised during the period	-
SARs granted during the period	136,569
SARs outstanding as of March 31, 2010	**243,060**
Of which: SARs exercisable at March 31, 2010	*104,638*
SARs forfeited during the period	(54,745)
SARs exercised during the period	-
SARs granted during the period	145,450
SARs outstanding as of March 31, 2011	**333,765**
Of which: SARs exercisable at March 31, 2011	*193,276*

The vesting conditions of the SARs granted by KLM on July 1, 2010, 2009 and 2008 are such that one third of the options vest at grant date, with a further one third after one and two years, respectively. Vesting is conditional on KLM achieving predetermined non-market-dependent performance criteria.

The fair value of the services provided under the SARs plan has been determined according to the market value of the Air France-KLM share at the closing date concerned:

+ for the July 2008 plan: a market value of €11.75 and a fair market value of €1.3 million;

+ for the July 2009 plan: a market value of €11.75 and a fair market value of €1.2 million;

+ for the July 2010 plan: a market value of €11.75 and a fair market value of €1.5 million.

28.5   Salary expenses related to share-based compensation

Year ended March 31, *(In € millions)*	Note	2011	2010
Shares-for-salary exchange 2003		25	25
Stock option plan		1	2
Salary expenses	**7**	**26**	**27**

Note 29 Provisions and retirement benefits

(In € millions)	Retirement benefits Note 29.1	Restitution of aircraft	Restructuring	Litigation	Others	Total
Amount as of March 31, 2009	**799**	**541**	**10**	**359**	**105**	**1,814**
Of which:						
◆ *non-current*	799	368	-	67	100	1,334
◆ *current*	-	173	10	292	5	480
New provision	149	201	191	30	80	651
Use of provision	(44)	(180)	(3)	(20)	(46)	(293)
Reversal of unnecessary provisions	-	(14)	(3)	(3)	-	(20)
Currency translation adjustment	1	-	-	-	-	1
Reclassification	14	(32)	-	(7)	-	(25)
Amount as of March 31, 2010	**919**	**516**	**195**	**359**	**139**	**2,128**
Of which:						
◆ *non-current*	919	345	1	38	129	1,432
◆ *current*	-	171	194	321	10	696
New provision	148	250	15	147	44	604
Use of provision	(86)	(166)	(86)	(103)	(38)	(479)
Reversal of unnecessary provisions	-	(15)	(2)	(2)	-	(19)
Currency translation adjustment	-	(3)	-	-	-	(3)
Change in scope	3	-	-	-	-	3
Discount/Accretion impact	-	(9)	-	-	-	(9)
Reclassification	2	(17)	-	-	7	(8)
Amount as of March 31, 2011	**986**	**556**	**122**	**401**	**152**	**2,217**
Of which:						
◆ *non-current*	986	414	-	382	148	1,930
◆ *current*	-	142	122	19	4	287

Movements in provisions for retirement benefits which have an impact on the income statement are recorded in "salaries and related costs".

As of March 31, 2011, the impact of the closure of a pension plan in the United States has been recorded in "Other non-current income and expenses" (see Note 10).

As of March 31, 2010, the impact of the Air France voluntary redundancy plan on "retirement benefits" has been recorded in "Other non-current income and expenses" (see Note 10).

Movements in provisions for restructuring which have an impact on the income statement are recorded in "other non-current income and expenses" when the plans concerned have a material impact.

Movements in provisions for restitution of aircraft which have an impact on the income statement are recorded in "provisions" except for the discount/accretion impact which is recorded in "other financial income and expenses".

Movements in provisions for litigation and in provisions for other risks and charges which have an impact on the income statement are recorded, depending on their nature, in the different lines of the income statement.

29.1 Retirement benefits

The Group holds a large number of retirement and other long-term benefits plans for its employees. The specific characteristics (benefit formulas, funding policies and types of assets held) of the plans vary according to the regulations and laws in the particular country in which the employees are located. Several of the plans are defined benefit plans.

Pension fund surplus

For a certain number of pension obligations, the Group funds pension funds.

The obligations of KLM group are, for the most part, funded in accordance with Dutch regulation and the Group's collective agreement. With regard to the level of coverage of the commitments, particularly for the pilots' program as well as that for the ground staff, significant "funding requirements" constraints force the Group to be always in a position of "over-funding".

Actuarial assumptions used

Actuarial valuations of the Group's benefit obligation were computed as of March 31, 2011 and 2010. These calculations include:

+ assumptions on staff turnover, life expectancy and salary increase;
+ assumptions of retirement age varying from 55 to 67 depending on the localization and the applicable laws;
+ discount rates used to determine the actuarial present value of the projected benefit obligations. The discount rates for each geographical area are determined according to the duration of each plan, taking into account the evolution of average interest rates on bonds rated AA market, observed on the main index available. In some countries, where the market regarding this type of bond is not large enough, the discount rate is determined with reference to bonds. Most of the Group's obligations are located in the Euro zone.

Year ended March 31,	2011	2010
Euro zone – Duration 4 to 5 years	4.25%	3.00%
Euro zone – Duration 10 to 15 years	4.75%	4.75%
Euro zone – Duration 15 years and more	5.35%	4.75%

The sensitivity of the annual cost and the obligation to variations in the discount rate is as follows:

(In € millions)	Sensitivity of the assumptions for the year ended March 31, 2011	Sensitivity of the assumptions for the year ended March 31, 2010
0.25% increase in the discount rate		
◆ Impact on the cost	(18)	(19)
◆ Impact on the obligation	(481)	(473)
0.25% decrease in the discount rate		
◆ Impact on the cost	19	30
◆ Impact on the obligation	481	473

+ The expected long-term rates of return on funded pension plans assets are as follows:

Year ended March 31,	2011	2010
Euro zone	Between 3.0% and 6.8%	Between 3.2% and 6.8%

The expected average long-term rates of return on plan assets have been determined based on the expected long-term rates of return of the different asset classes: equities, bonds, real estate or other, weighted according to the asset allocation strategy in these schemes.

The sensitivity of the annual cost to variations in the expected return for plan assets is as follows:

(In € millions)	Sensitivity of the assumptions for the year ended March 31, 2011	Sensitivity of the assumptions for the year ended March 31, 2010
0.25% increase in the expected return for plan assets		
◆ Impact on the cost	35	28
0.25% decrease in the expected return for plan assets		
◆ Impact on the cost	(35)	(28)

✦ Assumption on increase in healthcare costs:

Year ended March 31,	2011	2010
USA-Canada	Between 9.5% and 10.0%	Between 9.5% and 10.0%

The sensitivity of the annual cost and the obligation to variations in the healthcare costs of the schemes is as follows:

(In € millions)	Sensitivity of the assumptions for the year ended March 31, 2011	Sensitivity of the assumptions for the year ended March 31, 2010
1% increase in healthcare costs		
◆ Impact on the cost	-	-
◆ Impact on the obligation	5	4
1% decrease in healthcare costs		
◆ Impact on the cost	-	-
◆ Impact on the obligation	(5)	(4)

✦ On average, the main assumptions used in the actuarial valuations of obligations are summarized below:

Year ended March 31,	Pension benefits		Other benefits	
	2011	2010	2011	2010
Discount rate	5.14%	4.79%	5.42%	5.91%
Salary inflation rate	2.53%	2.60%	-	-
Expected long-term rate of return on plan assets	6.09%	6.19%	-	-

Changes in benefit obligations

The following table details the reconciliation between the benefits obligation and plan assets of the Group and the amounts recorded in the financial statements for the years ended March 31, 2011 and 2010.

(In € millions)	Pension benefits		Other benefits	
	2010-11	**2009-10**	**2010-11**	**2009-10**
Benefit obligation at beginning of year	**13,082**	**11,060**	**40**	**35**
Service cost	367	299	-	-
Interest cost	634	617	2	2
Employees' contribution	52	52	-	-
Plan amendments	-	(18)	-	-
Change of scope	3	(1)	-	1
Settlements/curtailments	(124)	(51)	-	-
Benefits paid	(503)	(543)	(2)	(3)
Transfers of assets/liability through Balance Sheet	(3)	-	-	-
Actuarial loss/(gain)	(245)	1,643	2	4
Currency translation adjustment	7	24	(2)	1
Benefit obligation at end of year	**13,270**	**13,082**	**40**	**40**
Including benefit obligation resulting from schemes totally or partly financed	*13,077*	*12,918*	*-*	*-*
Including not-financed benefit obligation	*193*	*164*	*40*	*40*
Fair value of plan assets at beginning of year	**13,487**	**11,031**	**-**	**-**
Actual return on plan assets	832	2,536	-	-
Employers' contributions	394	377	-	-
Employees' contributions	52	52	-	-
Change of scope	-	-	-	-
Settlements/curtailments	(111)	(4)	-	-
Transfers of assets/liability through Balance Sheet	(3)	-	-	-
Benefits paid	(482)	(525)	-	-
Currency translation adjustment	5	20	-	-
Fair value of plan assets at end of year	**14,174**	**13,487**	**-**	**-**

(In € millions)	Pension benefits		Other benefits	
	2010-11	2009-10	2010-11	2009-10
Funded status	904	405	(40)	(40)
Unrecognized prior service cost	164	182	-	-
Unrecognized actuarial (gains)/losses	977	1,264	4	3
Prepaid (accrued) pension cost	**2,045**	**1,851**	**(36)**	**(37)**
Amounts recorded in the balance sheet*:				
Pension asset (Note 21)	2,995	2,733	-	-
Provision for retirement benefits	(950)	(882)	(36)	(37)
Net amount recognized	**2,045**	**1,851**	**(36)**	**(37)**
Net periodic cost:				
Service cost	367	299	-	-
Interest cost	634	617	2	2
Expected return on plan assets	(836)	(682)	-	-
Settlement/curtailment	21	(36)	-	-
Amortization of prior service cost	18	21	-	-
Amortization of unrecognized actuarial (gain) loss	13	40	-	-
Other	-	8	-	-
Net periodic cost	**217**	**267**	**2**	**2**

*   *Except for those pension plans for which the balance is a net asset fully recorded as a non-current asset, all the obligations are recorded as non-current liabilities.*

The benefit obligations, fair value of plan assets and experience adjustments are as follows:

(In € millions)	Benefit obligations	Fair value of plan assets	Funded status	Experience adjustments on	
				Benefit obligation	Plan asset
As of March 31, 2007	11,636	13,404	1,768	230	207
As of March 31, 2008	10,909	13,176	2,267	(95)	(989)
As of March 31, 2009	11,095	11,031	(64)	(133)	(2,788)
As of March 31, 2010	13,122	13,487	365	95	1,854
As of March 31, 2011	13,310	14,174	864	47	(4)

Asset allocation

The weighted average allocation of the funds invested in Group pension plans as of March 31, 2011 and 2010 is as follows:

	Funds invested	
Year ended March 31,	**2011**	**2010**
Equities	40%	38%
Bonds	50%	52%
Real estate	10%	8%
Insurer assets	-	1%
Short-term investments	-	1%
Other	-	-
Total	**100%**	**100%**

Expected cash outflows

The table below shows the expected cash outflows on pensions and other post-employment benefits, as of March 31, 2011, over the next ten years:

(In € millions)	**Pensions and similar benefits**
Estimated contribution to be paid in 2011-12	*402*
Estimated benefit payments as of March 31:	
2012	509
2013	490
2014	513
2015	540
2016	571
2017-2021	3,330

Risks on pension obligation

Some Group's commitments are subject to an "over-hedging" which is determined both by the local regulations and the collective agreements. An evolution of the regulations could have a favorable or unfavorable impact on the commitments and/or level of coverage of these commitments.

The revision of IAS19 on pension obligations will have an impact on the equity of the Group. This amount will be determined when applying the revised standard whose terms and date of implementation are not yet final.

29.2 Other provisions

Provision for litigation with third parties

An assessment of litigation risks with third parties was carried out with the Group's attorneys and provisions have been recorded whenever circumstances rendered it necessary.

Provisions for litigation with third parties also include provisions for tax risks. Such provisions are set up when the Group considers that the tax authorities could challenge a tax position adopted by the Group or one of its subsidiaries.

In the normal course of its activities, the Air France-KLM group and its subsidiaries Air France and KLM (and their subsidiaries) are involved in litigation, some of which may be significant.

Provision for restructuring

As of March 31, 2011 and 2010, the provision for restructuring mainly includes the provision for the Air France voluntary redundancy plan (see Note 10).

Litigation concerning anti-trust laws

In the air-freight industry

a) Investigation of the anti-trust authorities

Air France, KLM and Martinair, a wholly-owned subsidiary of KLM since January 1, 2009, have been involved, since February 2006, with twenty-five other airlines in investigations initiated by the anti-trust authorities in several countries, with respect to allegations of anti-competitive agreements or concerted action in the air-freight industry.

The proceedings initiated in the United States, Australia and Canada resulted, during 2008-09 financial year, in Plea Agreements made by Air France, KLM and Martinair with the appropriate agencies, and the payment of fines putting an end to those proceedings. As of March 31, 2011 discussions were underway with the Competition Commission of South Africa to conclude a settlement agreement which would result in the payment by the Group of a penalty of €1.8 million.

In Europe, the European Commission announced, on November 9, 2010, its decision to impose fines on 14 airlines including Air France, KLM and Martinair related to anti-competition practices – mainly concerning fuel surcharges. The Commission imposed an overall fine of €340 million on the Air France-KLM group companies.

This fine exceeds, by €127 million, the provisions already made by the Group in its accounts. Consequently, an additional "non current expense" has been recorded.

As the Group's parent company, Air France-KLM was considered by the European Commission to be jointly and severally liable for the anti-competitive practices of which the Group companies were found guilty.

On January 24 and 25, 2011, the Group companies have filed an appeal against the decision before the General Court of European Union.

Since the appeal does not suspend the payment of the fines, the Group companies have chosen not to pay fine immediately, but to provide bank guarantees until a definitive ruling by the European Courts.

In South Korea on November 29, 2010, the Korean antitrust authority (KFTC) imposed on Air France-KLM, Air France and KLM a total fine of €8.6 million. The group companies have filed an appeal before the competent Court.

This fine will not impact the financial statements of the Group given that provisions have already been booked.

The total amount of provisions as of March 31, 2011 amounts to €365 million for all of the current proceedings.

b) Civil actions

As of March 31, 2011, the Group remains exposed in relation to class actions brought in Canada. With regard to the revenues involved, the risk is not significant.

Other provisions

Other provisions are mainly provisions for power-by-hour contracts (maintenance activity of the Group).

29.3 Contingent liabilities

The Group is involved in a number of governmental, legal and arbitrage procedures for which provisions have not been recorded in the financial statements.

Litigations concerning anti-trust laws

These litigations have not been provisioned given that the Group is unable, given the current status of proceedings, to evaluate its exposure.

a) In the air-freight industry

a.1) Investigation of the anti-trust authorities

The proceedings in Switzerland and Brazil, are still ongoing as of March 31, 2011.

With regard to the revenues involved, these risks are not individually significant.

a.2) Civil suits

Pursuant to the initiation in February 2006 of the various competition authority investigations, class actions were brought by forwarding agents and air-freight shippers in the United States and Canada against Air France, KLM and Martinair, and the other freight carriers.

In addition, civil suits have been filed in Europe by shippers following the European Commission's decision of November 9, 2010.

United States

In the United States, the Group concluded a Settlement Agreement with the representatives of the class action in July 2010. The Settlement Agreement, under which the Group accepted to pay USD 87 million, brings to a close all claims, lawsuits and legal proceedings in the past, present or future by plaintiffs seeking to obtain financial compensation from the Air France-KLM group for unlawful practices in freight transportation to, from or within the United States. The Settlement has no impact on the Group's financial statements, given the provisions already made to cover this risk.

On March 14, 2011, The Court issued an order granting final approval of the Air France-KLM settlement with the class action plaintiffs. Prior to that time, pursuant to procedures established by the Court, 36 entities elected to be excluded from the settlement, which permits them to separately pursue claims, but only four of those were customers of Air France, KLM or Martinair. In addition, a number of additional parties, including potentially one AF-KLM customer, filed a late exclusion notice and the Court has established a process to determine whether exclusion of those parties will be permitted.

With respect to those AF-KLM customers who have chosen to be excluded, a portion of the settlement proportional to the revenue AF-KLM received from those parties for a specified period as compared with Air France-KLM's overall revenue for that period will be segregated in a separate escrow. If claims by those parties, including written demands, are made against AF-KLM, then the portion of the separate escrow attributable to the claiming parties will be transferred to AF-KLM.

Netherlands

In the Netherlands, KLM, Martinair and Air France have been summoned on September 30, 2010, to appear before the District Court of Amsterdam in a civil suit brought by a company named Equilib which states that it has purchased claims from seventy purchasers of airfreight services who have allegedly suffered losses as a result of an anti-trust infringement in the European market between 2000 and 2006.

Equilib is seeking to obtain a declaratory judgment confirming that the Group companies have been guilty of unlawful conduct and are jointly and severally liable, along with other carriers, for the losses suffered by the airfreight purchasers. Equilib currently estimates its claims at €400 million but does not substantiate that figure.

The group companies served a contribution writ of summons on the other airlines fined by the European Commission on November 9, 2010.

United Kingdom

In the United Kingdom, a civil suit has been filed with the competent court in the UK against British Airways by two flower importers. British Airways issued contribution proceedings against all the airlines fined by the European Commission including entities of the Group.

The group companies will firmly resist all claims brought against them.

b) In the air transport industry (passengers)

b.1) Investigation of the European Commission into the air transport industry (passengers) between Europe and Japan

Air France and KLM, like other air carriers, were subject on March 11, 2008 to searches and seizures in connection with an investigation by the European Commission into possible anti-competitive agreements or concerted practices in the area of air transport services (passengers) between the States parties to the agreement on the European Economic Area and Japan.

On February 13, 2009, Air France and KLM replied to a questionnaire from the Commission pointing out the background of air traffic relations between France and the Netherlands, on the one hand, and Japan on the other hand. These relations are governed by bilateral agreements requiring the approval of fares by the civil aviation authorities in the States concerned after agreement among the air carriers designated pursuant to such agreements.

A second questionnaire was sent to the Group by the European Commission on October 1, 2009. To date, the Group is unable to state an opinion regarding the action that will be taken in connection with such enquiries by the European Commission.

b.2) Civil actions

During 2009, Air France and KLM were subpoenaed in a class action involving all the airlines operating transpacific routes between the United States and Asia/Oceania, on the basis of allegations of price-fixing on such routes.

Air France, which has only one transpacific route between the United States and Tahiti, and KLM, which is not involved on these routes, strongly deny these allegations. Both airlines accordingly filed motions to dismiss.

Other litigations

a) Pretory

Société Air France, as a legal entity, was placed under investigation on July 20, 2006 on charges of concealed employment and as an accessory to misuse of corporate assets in connection with a judicial investigation initiated against the officers of Pretory, a company with which Air France, pursuant to the September 2011 attacks, had entered into an agreement for the provision of safety officers on certain flights.

The airline immediately filed a motion with the Paris Court of Appeal for annulment of the implication in the investigation notified to it. Though that motion was denied, Société Air France intends to challenge its implication in this case.

b) KLM minority shareholders

On January 2008, the association VEB served KLM and Air France-KLM before the Amsterdam Civil Court claiming that KLM and Air France-KLM be ordered to pay out a higher dividend than the €0.58 per ordinary share paid for fiscal year 2007-08.

On September 1, 2010 the Court dismissed the case on the grounds that the dividend resolution met the test of reasonableness and fairness. VEB have appealed the Amsterdam Court decision.

c) Rio-Paris AF447 flight

Following to the crash of the Rio-Paris AF447 flight in the South Atlantic, a number of legal actions have been brought in the United States and Brazil by the victims' heirs.

All these proceedings are aimed at receiving damages as reparation for the losses suffered by the heirs of the passengers who died in the crash.

In the United States, all the proceedings have been consolidated in California before the Northern district Court.

On October 4, 2010, the District judge granted the defendants' motion for dismissal on grounds of "forum non convenience" and suggested that they pursue their claim in France. The damages as reparation for the losses suffered by the heirs of the passengers who died in the crash are covered by Air France's third-party liability insurance policy.

On March 17 and 18, 2011 respectively, Airbus and Air France were indicted for manslaughter by the investigating magistrate and incur the penalities of fines as prescribed by law. Air France intends to challenge its implication in this case.

To the best of Air France-KLM's knowledge, there is no other dispute, arbitration or non-recurring event that could have or has had in the recent past a significant impact on the Group's financial position, earnings or assets and liabilities.

Except for the matters specified under the paragraphs 29.2 and 29.3, the company is not aware of any governmental, judicial or arbitration proceedings (including any proceedings of which the issuer is aware, or that are pending or threatened against it) that could have or have recently had a significant impact on the issuer's and/or Group's financial position or profitability, during a period including at least the past twelve months.

Note 30 Financial debt

Year ended March 31, *(In € millions)*	2011	2010
Non current financial debt		
Perpetual subordinated loan stock in Yen	241	232
Perpetual subordinated loan stock in Swiss francs	325	296
OCEANE (convertible bonds)	984	964
Bonds	1,450	1,450
Capital lease obligations (non current portion)	3,059	3,421
Other debt (non current portion)	2,921	2,859
Total	**8,980**	**9,222**
Current financial debt		
Capital lease obligations (current portion)	695	579
Other debt (current portion)	994	1,131
Accrued interest	119	115
Total	**1,808**	**1,825**

30.8 Credit lines

As of March 31, 2011, the Group had credit lines amounting to €1,895 million, of which only €500 million have been drawn down. The three main credit lines amounted respectively, to €1,115 million for Air France, €530 million for KLM and €250 million for the holding Air France-KLM.

Air France's credit facility is subject to the respect of financial covenants, which were respected at March 31, 2011. It matures on April 7, 2012.

On April 4, 2011, Air France renewed this facility early with a 1,060 million revolving credit facility maturing on April 4, 2016, subject to the following financial covenants based on the Air France consolidated financial statements:

✦ EBITDAR must not be lower than two and a half times the net interest charges increased by one third of operating lease payments;
✦ non-current assets in the balance sheet, not pledged as collateral, must be at least equal to unsecured financial net debts.

These ratios are calculated every six months.

KLM's credit facility, which amounts to €530 million with a maturity in 2012, is subject to the respect of the following financial covenants calculated based on the KLM consolidated financial statements:

✦ EBITDAR must not be lower than two and a half times the sum of the net interest charges and one third of operating lease payments;
✦ Non-current assets in the balance sheet, not pledged as collateral, must be at least equal to 1.25 times the unsecured net debts.

These ratios are calculated every six months and were respected at March 31, 2011.

Air France-KLM's credit facility, which amounts to €250 million, with a maturity as of October 4, 2017 and reduced by €50 million per year starting 2013, is subject to respect of the following financial covenants calculated based on the Air France-KLM consolidated financial statements:

✦ the EBITDAR added to operating lease payments must be at least equal to one time and an half net interest charges added to one third of operating lease payments;
✦ non-current assets in the balance sheet, not pledged as collateral, must be at least equal to unsecured financial net debts.

These ratios are calculated every six months and were respected at March 31, 2011.

Note 31 Other liabilities

Year ended March 31, (In € millions)	2011		2010	
	Current	Non current	Current	Non current
Tax liabilities	463	-	388	-
Employee-related liabilities	867	-	834	-
Non current assets' payables	43	-	26	-
Derivative instruments	396	194	524	651
Deferred income	120	1	74	87
Other	797	77	751	80
Total	**2,686**	**272**	**2,597**	**818**

Derivative instruments comprise €36 million of currency hedges on financial debts as of March 31, 2011, all as non current liability (€39 million as of March 31, 2010 including a current portion of €13 million).

Note 32 Financial instruments

32.1 Risk management

Market risk management

Market risk coordination and management is the responsibility of the Risk Management Committee (RMC) which comprises the Chief Executive Officer and the Chief Financial Officer of Air France, the Chief Executive Officer and the Chief Financial Officer of KLM. The RMC meets each quarter to review Group reporting of the risks relating to the fuel price, the principal currency exchange rates and interest rates, and to decide on the hedging to be implemented: targets for hedging ratios, the time periods for the respect of these targets and, potentially, the preferred types of hedging instrument. The aim is to reduce the exposure of Air France-KLM and, thus, to preserve budgeted margins. The RMC also defines the counterparty-risk policy.

The decisions made by the RMC are implemented by the Treasury and Fuel Purchasing departments within each company, in compliance with the procedures governing the delegation of powers. In-house procedures governing risk management prohibit speculation.

The instruments used are swaps, furures and options.

Regular meetings are held between the Fuel Purchasing and Treasury departments of both companies in order to exchange information concerning matters such as hedging instruments used, strategies planned and counterparties.

The Cash Management departments of each company circulate information on the level of cash and cash equivalents to their respective executive managements on a daily basis. Every month, a detailed report including, amongst other information, interest rate and currency positions, the portfolio of hedging instruments, a summary of investments and financing by currency and the monitoring of risk by counterparty is transmitted to the executive managements.

The implementation of the policy on fuel hedging is the responsibility of the Fuel Purchasing departments, which are also in charge of purchasing fuel for physical delivery. A weekly report, enabling the evaluation of the net-hedged fuel cost of the current fiscal year and the two following ones, is supplied to the executive management. This mainly covers the transactions carried out during the week, the valuation of all positions, the hedge percentages as well as the breakdown of instruments and the underlyings used, average hedge levels, the resulting net prices and stess scenarii, as well as market commentary. Furthermore, the Fuel Purchasing departments makes a weekly Air France-KLM group report (known as the GEC report) which consolidates the figures from the two companies relating to fuel hedging and physical cost.

Currency risk

Most of the Group's revenues are generated in euros. However, because of its international activities, the Group incurs a foreign exchange risk. The principal exposure is to the US dollar, and then, to a lesser extent, to Japanese yen and pound sterling. Thus, any changes in the exchange rates for these currencies relative to the euro may have an impact on the Group's financial results. With regard to the US dollar, since expenditure or items such as fuel, operating leases and component costs exceed the level of revenue, the Group is a net buyer. This means that any significant appreciation in the dollar against the euro could result in a negative impact on the Group's activity and financial results.

Conversely, Air France-KLM is a net seller of the yen and of sterling, the level of revenues in these currencies exceeding expenditure.

As a result, any significant decline in these currencies relative to the euro could have a negative effect on the Group's activity and financial results. In order to reduce its currency exposure, the Group has adopted hedging strategies. Both companies progressively hedge their net exposure over a rolling 24 month period.

Aircraft are purchased in US dollars, meaning that the Group is highly exposed to a rise in the dollar against the euro for its aeronautics investments. The hedging policy plans the progressive and systematic implementation of hedging between the date of the aircraft order and their delivery date.

The exchange rate risk on the Group's financial debt is limited. At March 31, 2011, 88% of the Group's gross debt, after taking into account derivative instruments, was issued in or converted into euros, thereby sharply reducing the risk of currency fluctuations on the debt.

Despite this active hedging policy, not all exchange rate risks are covered. The Group and its subsidiaries might then encounter difficulties in managing currency risks, which could have a negative impact on the Group's business and financial results.

Interest rate risk

At both Air France and KLM, most financial debt is contracted in floating-rate instruments in line with market practice. However, given the historically low level of interest rates, Air France and KLM have used swap strategies to convert a significant proportion of their floating-rate debt into fixed rates. After swaps, the Air France-KLM group's gross debt contracted at fixed rates represents 71% of the overall total. Given this policy, the Group displays an amount of floating-rate debt lower than the amount of floating-rate treasury. An interest rate increase will consequently have a positive effect on the Group's financial results.

This page has been intentionally left blank

Commodity risk linked to fuel prices

In the normal course of its business, the Group conducts transactions on petroleum product markets in order to effectively manage the risks related to the purchases of fuel.

The nominal amounts of the Group's commitments on the crude and refined oil markets are shown below:

➤ Year ended March 31, 2011

(In € millions)	Nominal	Maturity below 1 year	Maturities between 1 and 5 years					Fair value
			1-2 years	2-3 years	3-4 years	4-5 years	+ 5 years	
Commodity risk (cash flow hedging operating flows)	**5,795**	**3,956**	**1,839**	-	-	-	-	**538**
Swap	124	124	-	-	-	-	-	29
Options	5,671	3,832	1,839	-	-	-	-	509
Commodity risk (trading)	-	-	-	-	-	-	-	-
Swap	-	-	-	-	-	-	-	-
Options	-	-	-	-	-	-	-	-
Total	**5,795**	**3,956**	**1,839**	-	-	-	-	**538**

➤ Year ended March 31, 2010

(In € millions)	Nominal	Maturity below 1 year	Maturities between 1 and 5 years					Fair value
			1-2 years	2-3 years	3-4 years	4-5 years	+ 5 years	
Commodity risk (cash flow hedging operating flows)	**5,214**	**3,252**	**1,242**	**720**	-	-	-	**(646)**
Swap	92	92	-	-	-	-	-	3
Options	5,122	3,160	1,242	720	-	-	-	(649)
Commodity risk (trading)	**32**	**32**	-	-	-	-	-	**(4)**
Swap	-	-	-	-	-	-	-	-
Options	32	32	-	-	-	-	-	(4)
Total	**5,246**	**3,284**	**1,242**	**720**	-	-	-	**(650)**

Within the framework of cash flow hedges, maturities relate to realization dates of hedged items. Therefore, amounts of fair value presented in stockholders' equity are recycled in income at realization dates of hedged items.

32.3   Market value of financial instruments

Market values are estimated for most of the Group's financial instruments using a variety of valuation methods, such as discounted future cash flows. However, the methods and assumptions used to provide the information set out below are theoretical in nature. They bear the following inherent limitations:

+ estimated market values cannot take into consideration the effect of subsequent fluctuations in interest or exchange rates;
+ estimated amounts as of March 31, 2011 and 2010 are not indicative of gains and/or losses arising upon maturity or in the event of cancellation of a financial instrument.

The application of alternative methods and assumptions may, therefore, have a significant impact on the estimated market values.

The methods used are as follows:

+ *Cash, trade receivables, other receivables, short-term bank facilities, trade payables and other payables:*
The Group believes that, due to their short-term nature, net book value can be deemed a reasonable approximation of market value.

+ *Marketable securities, investments and other securities:*

The market value of securities is determined based mainly on the market price or the prices available on other similar securities.

Where no comparable exists, the Group uses their book value, which is deemed a reasonable approximation of market value in this instance.

+ *Borrowings, other financial debts and loans:*
The market value of fixed and floating-rate loans and financial debts is determined based on discounted future cash flows at market interest rates for instruments with similar features.

+ *Derivatives instruments:*
The market value of derivatives instruments corresponds to the amounts payable or receivable were the positions to be closed out as of March 31, 2011 and 2010 calculated using the year-end market rate.

Market values calculated in this way are shown in the table below:

(In € millions)	March 31, 2011		March 31, 2010	
	Net book value	Estimated market value	Net book value	Estimated market value
Financial assets				
Financial assets available for sale				
Shares	977	977	54	54
Assets at fair value through profit and loss				
Marketable securities	574	574	343	343
Loans and receivables				
Loans				
Fixed-rate	216	229	299	323
Floating-rate	117	117	115	113
Interest rate derivative instruments				
Interest rate swaps	15	15	15	15
Exchange rate derivative instruments				
Exchange rate options	(16)	(16)	88	88
Forward currency contracts	58	58	126	126
Currency swaps	-	-	-	-
Commodity derivative instruments				
Petroleum swaps and options	889	889	280	280
Trade accounts receivables	1,938	1,938	2,142	2,142
Other assets (except derivatives instruments)	760	760	650	650

(In € millions)	March 31, 2011		March 31, 2010	
	Net book value	Estimated market value	Net book value	Estimated market value
Cash and cash equivalents				
Cash equivalents	3,343	3,343	3,294	3,294
Cash in hand	374	374	457	457
Financial liabilities				
Debt measured at amortized cost				
Bonds*				
Fixed-rate	2,434	2,822	2,414	2,859
Perpetual subordinated loans	566	594	528	536
Other borrowings and financial debt				
Fixed-rate	2,164	2,176	2,178	2,123
Variable-rate	5,624	5,531	5,927	5,818
Derivatives				
Interest rate derivative instruments				
Interest rate swaps	76	76	141	141
Exchange derivative instruments				
Exchange rate options	46	46	27	27
Forward currency contracts	114	114	76	76
Currency swaps	3	3	1	1
Commodity derivative instruments				
Petroleum swaps and options	351	351	930	930
Other debt				
Trade accounts payable	2,211	2,211	2,032	2,032
Deferred revenue on ticket sales	2,440	2,440	2,340	2,340
Frequent flyer programs	806	806	840	840
Other liabilities (except derivatives instruments)	2,368	2,368	2,240	2,240

* *The fixed rate bonds comprise the OCEANE (convertible bonds) issued in April 2005 and in June 2009, as well as €750 million of bonds issued in September 2006 and April 2007 by Air France and €700 million of bonds issued in October 2009 by Air France-KLM.*

OCEANE issued in April 2005: The market value of €475 million, was determined based on the bond's market price as of March 31, 2011. This market value includes the fair value of the debt component (amount of €402 million in the financial statements as of March 31, 2011) as well as the fair value of the conversion option recorded in equity for €48 million.

OCEANE issued in June 2009: The market value of €866 million, was determined based on the bond's market price as of March 31, 2011. This market value includes the fair value of the debt component (amount of €583 million in the financial statements as of March 31, 2011) as well as the fair value of the conversion option recorded in equity for €78 million.

Bond issued in September 2006 and April 2007: the characteristics of this bond are described in Note 30.3. The market value is €758 million.

Bond issued in October 2009: the characteristics of this bond are described in Note 30.3. The market value is €723 million.

32.4 Valuation methods for financial assets and liabilities at their fair value

The breakdown of the Group's financial assets and liabilities is as follows based on the three classification level (see Note 3.10.7):

As of March 31 (In € millions)	Level 1		Level 2		Level 3		Total	
	2011	2010	2011	2010	2011	2010	2011	2010
Financial assets available for sale								
Shares	941	15	36	39	-	-	977	54
Assets at fair value through profit and loss								
Marketable securities	7	-	567	343	-	-	574	343
Cash equivalents	3,343	3,294	-	-	-	-	3,343	3,294
Derivative instruments asset								
Interest rate derivatives	-	-	15	15	-	-	15	15
Currency exchange derivatives	-	-	43	214	-	-	43	214
Commodity derivatives	-	-	888	280	-	-	888	280

Financial liabilities at fair value comprise negative values of derivative instruments of interest rates, foreign exchange and commodities as well as the debt revalued in accordance with fair value hedge, valuations classified as level 2.

32.5 Sensitivity

The sensitivity is calculated solely on the valuation of derivatives at the closing date of each period presented.

The range of shocks has been judged reasonable and realistic by the Group's management. The shock assumptions used are coherent with those applied in the prior period.

The impact on equity corresponds to the sensitivity of effective fair value variations for instruments documented in the hedged cash flow (options intrinsic value, fair value of closed instruments). The impact on the income statement corresponds to the sensitivity of ineffective fair value variations of hedged instruments (principally time value of options) and fair value variations of transaction instruments.

For fuel and currency, the downward and upward sensitivities are not symmetrical when taking into account the utilization, in respect of the policy of optional hedging instruments whose risk profile is not linear.

Fuel hedge sensitivity
The impact on "income before tax" and on the "gains/(losses) taken to equity" of a +/- USD 10 variation in the price of a barrel of Brent is presented below:

(In € millions)	March 31, 2011		March 31, 2010	
	Increase of USD 10 per barrel of Brent	Decrease of USD 10 per barrel of Brent	Increase of USD 10 per barrel of Brent	Decrease of USD 10 per barrel of Brent
Income before tax	50	(78)	(121)	122
Gains/(losses) taken to equity	321	(309)	586	(582)

This page has been intentionally left blank

Note 33 Lease commitments

33.1 Capital leases

The debt related to capital leases is detailed in Note 30.

33.2 Operating leases

The minimum future payments on operating leases are as follows:

Year ended March 31, *(In € millions)*	Minimum lease payments	
	2011	**2010**
Flight equipment		
Due dates		
Y+1	821	807
Y+2	801	665
Y+3	670	562
Y+4	528	458
Y+5	449	388
Over 5 years	1,381	1,234
Total	**4,650**	**4,113**
Buildings		
Due dates		
Y+1	223	203
Y+2	184	191
Y+3	160	185
Y+4	149	179
Y+5	125	159
Over 5 years	983	1,036
Total	**1,824**	**1,953**

The expense relating to operating leases for flight equipment amounted to €831 million for the year ended March 31, 2011 and to €721 million for the year ended March 31, 2010.

The Group may sub-lease flight equipment and buildings. The revenue generated by this activity is not significant for the Group.

39.2 Equity affiliates

Entity	Country	Segment	% interest	% control
AIRCRAFT CAPITAL Ltd	United Kingdom	Other	40	40
AEROLIS	France	Passenger	50	50
ALITALIA	Italy	Passenger	25	25
FINANCIÈRE LMP	France	Passenger	40	40
HEATHROW CARGO HANDLING	United Kingdom	Cargo	50	50
CSC INDIA	India	Cargo	49	49
AEROSTRUCTURES MIDDLE EAST SERVICES	United Arab Emirates	Maintenance	50	50
AEROTECHNIC INDUSTRIES	Morocco	Maintenance	50	50
SPAIRLINERS	Germany	Maintenance	50	50
COTONOU CATERING	Benin	Other	24	49
DOUAL'AIR	Cameroon	Other	25	25
FLYING FOOD CATERING	United States	Other	48	49
FLYING FOOD JFK	United States	Other	48	49
FLYING FOOD MIAMI	United States	Other	48	49
FLYING FOOD SAN FRANCISCO	United States	Other	43	44
FLYING FOOD SERVICES	United States	Other	48	49
FLYING FOOD SERVICES USA	United States	Other	49	49
GUANGHOU NANLAND CATERING COMPANY	China	Other	24	25
INTERNATIONAL AEROSPACE MANAGEMENT COMPANY S.C.R.L.	Italy	Other	20	20
KENYA AIRWAYS LIMITED	Kenya	Other	26	26
LOGAIR	France	Other	49	50
LOME CATERING SA	Togo	Other	17	35
MACAU CATERING SERVICES	Macao	Other	17	34
MAINPORT INNOVATION FUND N.V.	Netherlands	Other	25	25
NEWREST SERVAIR UK LTD	United Kingdom	Other	39	40
PRIORIS	France	Other	33	34
SCHIPOL LOGISTICS PARK C.V.	Netherlands	Other	52	53
SERVAIR EUREST	Spain	Other	34	35
SKY ENERGY B.V.	Netherlands	Other	30	30
TERMINAL ONE GROUPE ASSOCIATION	United States	Other	25	25

5.7 Statutory Auditors' report on the consolidated financial statements

Year ended March 31, 2011

To the Shareholders,

In compliance with the assignment entrusted by your Annual General Meetings, we hereby report to you, for the year ended March 31, 2011, on:

+ the audit of the accompanying consolidated financial statements of Air France-KLM S.A.;
+ the justification of our assessments;
+ the specific verification required by law.

These consolidated financial statements have been approved by the Board of Directors. Our role is to express an opinion on these financial statements based on our audit.

▊ Opinion on the consolidated financial statements

We conducted our audit in accordance with professional standards applicable in France. Those standards require that we plan and perform the audit to obtain reasonable assurance about whether the consolidated financial statements are free of material misstatement. An audit involves performing procedures, using sampling techniques or other methods of selection, to obtain evidence about the amounts and disclosures in the consolidated financial statements. An audit also includes evaluating the appropriateness of accounting policies used and the reasonableness of accounting estimates made, as well as the overall presentation of the consolidated financial statements. We believe that the audit evidence we have obtained is sufficient and appropriate to provide a basis for our audit opinion.

In our opinion, the consolidated financial statements give a true and fair view of the assets and liabilities and of the financial position of the Group as at March 31, 2011 and of the results of its operations for the year then ended in accordance with IFRSs as adopted by the EU.

Without qualifying the above opinion, we draw your attention to Note 3.1 to the consolidated financial statements relating to the implementation of new IFRS standards and interpretations effective April 1, 2010.

▊ Justification of assessments

In accordance with the requirements of Article L. 823-9 of the French Commercial Code ("*Code de commerce*") relating to the justification of our assessment, we bring to your attention the following matters:

+ Notes 3.2, 3.14 and 17 to the consolidated financial statements describe the estimates and assumptions that Air France-KLM's management was required to make regarding the impairment tests of tangible assets. We have examined the data and assumptions on which these impairment tests were based as well as the procedures for implementing impairment tests, as described in the notes.
+ Air France-KLM's management is required to make estimates and assumptions relating to the recognition of revenue arising from issued but unused tickets and its Frequent Flyer Program, in accordance with the terms and conditions described in Notes 3.2, 3.6 and 3.7 to the consolidated financial statements. Our procedures consisted in analyzing the data used, assessing the assumptions made and reviewing the calculations performed.
+ Notes 3.17 and 29.1 to the consolidated financial statements specify the accounting policies for employee benefits. These benefits and obligations were evaluated by external actuaries. Our procedures consisted in examining the data used, assessing the assumptions made and verifying that the information included in Note 29.1 to the consolidated financial statements was appropriate. In addition, Note 3.17 to the consolidated financial statements outlines the accounting policies applied for the recognition of the pension fund surplus. We verified that this accounting treatment was appropriate.
+ Note 29.2 and 29.3 to the consolidated financial statements describes the anti-trust litigations to which the company is exposed and the amount of the related provision accounted for. Our procedures consisted in analyzing the method used to determine these provisions, examining the data used and the assumptions made, based on information available to date, and verifying that the information as disclosed in Note 29.2 and 29.3 to the consolidated financial statements was appropriate.

These assessments were made as part of our audit of the consolidated financial statements taken as a whole and therefore contributed to the opinion we formed which is expressed in the first part of this report.

▌ Specific procedures

As required by law we have also verified, in accordance with professional standards applicable in France, the information presented in the Group's management report.

We have no matters to report as to its fair presentation and its consistency with the consolidated financial statements.

Paris La Défense and Neuilly-sur-Seine, May 31, 2011
The Statutory Auditors

KPMG Audit
Division of KPMG S.A.

Valérie Besson
Partner

Michel Piette
Partner

Deloitte & Associés

Dominique Jumaucourt
Partner

This is a free translation into English of the Statutory Auditors' reports on the consolidated financial statements issued in the French language and is provided solely for the convenience of English speaking readers.

The Statutory Auditors' report includes information specifically required by French law in such report, whether qualified or not. This information is presented below the audit opinion on consolidated financial statements and includes explanatory paragraph discussing the auditors' assessments of certain significant accounting and auditing matters. These assessments were made for the purpose of issuing an audit opinion on the consolidated financial statements taken as a whole and not to provide separate assurance on individual account captions or on information taken outside of the consolidated financial statements.

This report also includes information relating to the specific verification of information given in the Group's management report. This report should be read in conjunction with and construed in accordance with French law and professional auditing standards applicable in France.

This page has been intentionally left blank

Glossaries

Air transport glossary

AEA
Association of European Airlines. Created in 1952, notably by Air France and KLM, the AEA represents the interests of its members within the European Union institutions, the European Civil Aviation Conference and other organizations and associations.

Available seat-kilometers (ASK)
Total number of seats available for the transportation of passengers multiplied by the number of kilometres traveled.

Available ton-kilometers (ATK)
Total number of tons available for the transportation of cargo, multiplied by the number of kilometres traveled.

Biometry
Technique allowing the identity of an individual to be verified, while crossing a national border for example, through the automatic recognition of certain pre-recorded physical characteristics.

Coordinated airport
Airport where a coordinator has been appointed to allocate landing and take off slots according to rules established in advance. All large European Union airports are coordinated.

Cabotage
Airline cabotage is the carriage of air traffic that originates and terminates within the boundaries of a given country by an air carrier of another country.

Capacity
Capacity is measured in available seat-kilometers.

Catering
In-flight catering involves the planning and preparation of meals and the assembly of meal trays destined to be served on board an aircraft.

Code share
In accordance with a code share agreement, two partner airlines offer services on the same aircraft, each under their own brand, their own IATA code and their own flight number. Code sharing may take two forms. In the first case, the two airlines purchase and sell seats to and from each other at an agreed price. The airline which has purchased the seats then markets them under its brand and at its fares. In the second case, under the system known as *free flow,* the two airlines are allowed to sell all the seats on the flights involved. Each airline retains the revenues generated on the flight it operates and remunerates the other airline for the number of seats the latter has sold on its aircraft.

Combi
Aircraft whose main deck is equipped for the transportation of both passengers and cargo. The freight is stored at the back of the aircraft and is accessed by a specially-fitted cargo door.

Connecting traffic
Traffic between two destinations which are not linked by a direct flight.

DGAC
Direction Générale de l'Aviation Civile. Under the authority of the French Ministry of Transport, the DGAC is in charge of the security of air transport and of air space in France.

DGTL
Directoraat-Generaal Transport en Luchtvaart. Under the authority of the Dutch Ministry of Traffic and Public Works, the DGTL is in charge of the security of air transport and of air space in the Netherlands.

E-services
Range of ground services offered by Air France and KLM to their passengers, based on new information technologies. E-services notably enable passengers to check in using self-service kiosks or via the airlines' websites as well as the use of electronic tickets.

EASA
European Aviation Safety Agency. EASA develops safety and environmental protection expertise in civil aviation in order to assist the European institutions to establish legislation and implement measures regarding aircraft security, organizations and associated staff.

Electronic ticketing
All the journey information for one or several passengers which, instead of being printed, is recorded in an airline's IT database, once the reservation has been made and paid for. An electronic or e-ticket replaces the traditional paper ticket.

Equivalent available seat-kilometer (EASK)
Measure of production after conversion of cargo tons into equivalent available seats.

Equivalent revenue passenger-kilometers (ERPK)

Overall measure of traffic after conversion of cargo tons into equivalent revenue passenger-kilometers.

Fare combinability

System which, on destinations served by both Air France and KLM, enables customers to choose between a journey with an onward flight connection at KLM's Schiphol hub and a journey with an onward flight connection at Air France's Roissy-Charles de Gaulle hub. With fare combinability, customers benefit from a choice of more frequencies via one or other of the hubs, for both the inbound and outbound trips. The fare is based on two half return tickets.

FAA

Federal Aviation Administration. Body responsible for civil aviation security in the United States.

Handling

Preparation of the aircraft, involving loading and unloading, as well as the associated logistics such as management and storage of hotel products.

High contribution

Fare classes corresponding to business or first class.

Hub

Term used for a transfer platform where departures and arrivals are scheduled to minimize transit times. Air France-KLM disposes of two of the four major European hubs: Roissy-Charles de Gaulle and Amsterdam-Schiphol. The Air France and KLM hubs are organized into successive waves for arrivals and departures each day in order to increase the transfer opportunities for customers.

IATA

International Air Transport Association. Created in 1945, IATA establishes regulations for the air transport industry and provides its members with a framework for the coordination and proper implementation of tariffs, together with various commercial and financial support services.

IATA year

Financial year which runs from April 1 to March 31 the following year.

ICAO

The International Civil Aviation Organisation, a UN Specialized Agency, promotes the safe, secure and sustainable development of civil aviation world-wide. It establishes the standards and regulations required to ensure the safety, security, efficiency and continuity of aviation operations as well as the protection of the environment.

Joint-venture

Joint company with two partners, often held equally with 50% each. This type of shareholder structure notably allows the implementation of technological or industrial alliances in order to undertake specific projects common to both partner companies.

Load factor

Revenue passenger-kilometers (RPK) divided by available seat-kilometers (ASK). In the cargo activity this is revenue ton-kilometers (RTK) divided by available ton-kilometers (ATK).

Multi-hub

System linking several hubs, allowing customers to access the networks developed from each hub, thus multiplying the round-trip offer to and from world-wide destinations.

Over-reservation or over-booking

Over-reservation or over-booking consists of accepting more bookings than seats available. Practiced by all airline companies and permitted by European legislation, this allows many passengers per year to find a seat on board aircraft by freeing up additional seats. Airlines usually have a passenger compensation policy.

Point-to-point traffic

Traffic between two airports, excluding all passengers prolonging their trip with a connecting flight.

Revenue management

Technique designed to optimize revenue on flights, by constantly seeking a better balance between the load factor and the fares offered.

Revenue per passenger per kilometer

Unit revenue for one paying passenger carried over one kilometer.

Revenue per ton per kilometer

Unit revenue for one ton of cargo carried over one kilometer.

⬚ Revenue passenger-kilometer (RPK)

Total number of paying passengers carried multiplied by the number of kilometers traveled.

⬚ Revenue ton-kilometer (RTK)

Total number of tons of paid cargo multiplied by the number of kilometers that this cargo is carried.

⬚ Safety and security

Airline safety includes all the measures implemented by air transport professionals aimed at ensuring the reliable operating and maintenance of aircraft.

Airline security involves all the measures taken by air transport professionals to prevent any illicit or malicious act. Air transport is particularly exposed to terrorist acts due to the considerable media impact offered by such activity. Airline security notably includes baggage screening, and the screening and questioning of passengers.

⬚ Summer season

Defined by IATA as the period running from the last Saturday in March to the last Saturday in October. The summer season corresponds to a schedule of summer flights over a period of seven months.

⬚ Self-service check-in kiosk

Self-service check-in kiosks, available in airport departure halls, allow passengers to check in and print their own boarding cards, without having to go to a check-in counter.

⬚ Segment

Section of a flight between two destinations. The number of passengers is calculated by segment carried.

⬚ Slot

A slot represents clearance given for a carrier to land at or take off from an airport at a specified time and date.

⬚ Sub-fleet

All the aircraft of the same type, with identical technical and commercial characteristics (engines, cabin configuration, etc.).

⬚ Ton-kilometers transported

Total number of tons transported multiplied by the number of kilometer covered.

⬚ Traffic

Traffic is measured in revenue passenger-kilometers.

⬚ Unit revenue

In the passenger business, corresponds to the revenue for one available seat or for one paying passenger transported over one kilometer. In the cargo business, corresponds to the revenue for one available ton or one ton transported over one kilometer.

⬚ Winter season

Defined by IATA as the period running from the first Sunday following the last Saturday in October to the Friday before the last Saturday in March. The winter season corresponds to a schedule of winter flights over five months.